How to Identify, Interview & Interrogate Child Abuse Offenders

David M. Buckley

Dedication:

To my wife Gina, whose love and support made this book possible and our four children, Nick, Tony, Bridget, and Brandon the most important people in our lives.

Library of Congress Control Number: 2006923584
ISBN 13: 978-0-9760093-5-1
ISBN 10: 0-9760093-5-8

John E. Reid and Associates, Inc.
209 West Jackson Boulevard, Suite 400, Chicago, IL 60606
www.Reid.com

Published and Printed by Hahn Printing Incorporated
752 North Adams Road, Eagle River, Wisconsin 54521

First Edition, First Printing

Table of Contents

Part One

Interviews of Convicted Child Abuse Offenders

Part Two

Practical Guidelines for Identifying, Interviewing and Interrogating Child Abuse Offenders

---

Appendices

Preface

John E. Reid & Associates, Inc. is a private corporation located in Chicago, Illinois. The company was founded by John Reid in 1947 following a distinguished eleven-year career as a Chicago police officer. The firm offers detection of deception services along with a variety of training programs in the art of interviewing and interrogation to clients in law enforcement, private companies, government agencies, and the legal community. The company has developed an international reputation as the leading expert in the field of interviewing and interrogation and trains thousands of investigators each year at our seminars conducted throughout the United States, Canada, Europe, and Asia.

Mr. Reid was actively engaged in the art of criminal interrogation for 40 years. A close friend and colleague, Professor Fred Inbau, once said of Mr. Reid that he was a "friendly, kind, and considerate man who had the ability to sit down alone with a murder or child rapist and not display any hatred toward that person. He had an understanding of the frailty of human beings, which became apparent to the suspect, and made it easier for them to confess to him rather than to someone who was exhibiting feelings of hate or disgust." Throughout his career Mr. Reid insisted that investigators treat suspects with decency and respect and never engage in any behavior that might provoke a confession from an innocent person. Mr. Reid left a legacy of exceedingly well-qualified interrogators who have continued to develop, improve and refine this structured approach to interviewing and interrogation which has become known as "The Reid Technique® of Interviewing and Interrogation."

In 1990 John E. Reid & Associates, Inc. introduced a specialized training program, developed by the author, called "Investigative Interviewing Techniques for Child Abuse Investigations." The practical guidelines and techniques presented in this program are designed to help investigators identify, interview and interrogate child abuse offenders. This book reflects many of the concepts presented in this training seminar and is intended for anyone involved in the investigation of child abuse cases, including law enforcement, social workers, clinicians, physicians and counselors.

I would like to thank Joseph P. Buckley, President of John E. Reid &Associates, Inc., for his assistance in editing this book and Brian C. Jayne, Director of Research and Development, for his input in the development of the investigative interviewing techniques presented in the book. I would also like to thank Holly S. Oehrlein, Esquire; Children's Justice Act Program Coordinator for the Virginia Department of Criminal Justice Services, for her contributions to the content of this book.

Due to the special nature of this book, with its discourse between investigator and suspect, the words *he* and *him* are used generically in order to avoid redundancy. Also the use of the words *alleged offender*, *suspect* and *subject* are generic terms used interchangeably throughout the book and refer to a person who is being interviewed. The reference to terms such as *"guilty," "innocent," "truthful" or "deceptive"* throughout the book refers to the opinion of the investigator based on his analysis of the investigative information.

Introduction

Child abuse is one of the most difficult and heart-wrenching crimes to investigate. Despite the tireless efforts of dedicated investigators, many cases are unsolved because of insufficient evidence to secure a conviction. Consequently, many abused children remain in the environment where they continue to be abused. Unlike most criminal investigations, victims of child abuse are either reluctant or unable to disclose the details of the crime or identify the offender.[1] According to the National Institute of Mental Health, an offender who sexually molests girls will have about 50 victims before being caught while an offender who sexually molests boys may have as many as 150 victims before being apprehended. Many victims are reluctant to report abuse because they feel a sense of shame or embarrassment while others may feel responsible for the abuse and do not want to be held responsible for breaking up the family or having the offender jailed. Some victims fear others will question the credibility of their allegation or blame them for the abusive behavior, while some victims are unaware of the fact that they have been abused.

---

[1] Only 42% of abused girls and 33% of abused boys disclose sexual abuse. Finkelhor, D., Hotaling, G., Lewis, I. A., & Smith C. (1990). Sexual abuse in a national survey of adult men and women: Prevalence, characteristics and risk factors. Child Abuse and Neglect, 14, 19-28.

Child abuse offenders are cognizant of the fact that the lack of physical evidence linking them to the abuse reduces the likelihood of a conviction even when the victim has identified him as the offender. Absent physical evidence or witnesses the investigator must rely on the victim's statement which often makes up the foundation of the case. Inconsistencies in the victim's statement can present problems prosecuting the case. Children between the ages of three and nine do not have a well-developed sense of time and may be unable to accurately identify when the abuse occurred or how many times they were abused.[2] Research has shown that the overall accuracy of a child's memory will deteriorate over time.[3] This affords the defense attorney an opportunity to point out these inconsistencies and attack the overall credibility of the child's statement. Therefore it is incumbent upon the investigator to enhance their interviewing and interrogation skills to identify the guilty offender and elicit the truth from them. A confession by the offender can save the victim from the trauma of further abuse and the stress that can be caused by the very system that is designed to protect them.

The first step in this investigative process is to take a glimpse into the mind of the child abuse offender. Offenders have a distorted perception of their behavior and often view themselves as the victim. They may consider themselves a victim of society, alcohol, their spouse, drugs, the victim's behavior, or their own inability to control their

---

[2] Walker, A. G. PhD. (1994) Handbook On Questioning Children : A linguistic Perspective

[3] Rhona Flin et al., The Effect of a Five-Month Delay on Children's and Adults' Eyewitness Memory, 83 Brit. 1. Psychology 323, 333 (1992).

emotional state. Looking at child abuse through the eyes of the offender will reveal how offenders select their victims, blame their victims, manipulate their victims, groom their victims and setup their victims. The reader will also learn from offenders how they justify, rationalize, and minimize their abusive behavior. This understanding is a prerequisite for the development of effective interview questions and a successful interrogation strategy. Investigators will become more effective eliciting the truth from offenders once they are able to see the offense through the eyes of the offender.

In an effort to provide investigators with insight into the mind of an offender, eight separate interviews of convicted child abuse offenders will be presented in Part One of this book. Their candor, which is sometimes unpleasantly graphic, will shed some light on how the mind of an offender works. All of the offenders, both male and female, presented in part one were incarcerated and participating in a sexual offender treatment program at the time of the interviews. Each offender volunteered to participate in this project and did not receive any compensation for their involvement. The author was not provided any advanced information about the offenders prior to their interviews and was not allowed to challenge any of their statements. Prior to their incarceration none of the offenders confessed their crime to authorities. The offenders were convicted based on the testimony of their victims or they entered into a plea bargain arrangement based on the advice of their attorney. Pseudonyms were used for the names of the victims and the offenders will be referred to by number. The details of each offender's statements are accurately represented. However, the interviews were edited into narrative segments rather than in the original question-and-answer format to present the information in a more concise manner for the reader. These interviews will then be used as illustrations in Part Two of this book to develop the investigative interviewing and interrogation techniques that have proven to be effective in developing valuable information and confessions from child abuse offenders.

Part One

Chapter 1

Child Abuse Offender Interviews

Introducing the offenders

The National Center for Post-Traumatic Stress Disorder estimates that 80% of sexual offenders are male and about 20% of sexual offenders are female. The 1999 U.S. Department of Health and Human Services report on child maltreatment reported that 89% of sexual offenders are male and only 11% are female. Bass and Davis estimate that 95% of offenders who sexually molest girls and 80% of offenders who sexually molest boys are male.[4] Consequently most child abuse research has focused on adult male offenders and therefore little is known about female offenders.[5] Sexual abuse by a female is easily masked by the woman's traditional role as the

---

[4] Bass, E., Davis, L. (1998) The Courage to Heal: A Guide for Woman Survivors of Child Sexual Abuse. Harper & Row 1998 p. 96

[5] Lewis, C.C & Stanlsy, C.R. (2000). Women accused of sexual offenses. Behavioral Sciences and the Law, 18, 73-81.

caregiver. A woman may conceal the sexual abuse of a child under the guise of attending to the child's hygiene. A young boy who is sexualized by an adult female may be considered "lucky" by today's societal standards.[6] There is increasing attention in today's media regarding female offenders. Several well-publicized cases involving female teachers accused of sexually molesting male students have drawn attention to the female offender. Even though female sexual offenders represent a small percentage of the offender population, four interviews of female child abuse offenders will be included in Part One along with the interviews of four male child abuse offenders to provide the reader unique insight into the mind of both male and female child abuse offenders.

The following descriptions will serve to introduce the eight offenders whose interviews are presented in Part One of this book:

Offender #1 is a 56-year-old white male. He has been married three times and has five children, three boys and two girls ranging in age from 21 to 31 years old. He is currently married to his third wife of one year. He is a former school teacher who taught third, fourth and fifth grades for about ten years. He admits to molesting 48 of his female students, none of whom reported the abuse. He also admits kidnapping a nine-year-old girl who he sexually assaulted and then released. He was never arrested for that offense. Following the kidnapping he was arrested and convicted for indecent exposure and attempted sexual assault on

---

[6] Anderson, P.B. & Struckman-Johnson, C. (Eds.) (1998). Sexually aggressive women: Current perspectives and controversies. New York: The Guilford Press.

another nine-year-old girl for which he served eighteen months. At the time of his interview he was serving a sentence for molesting another ten-year-old girl.

Offender #2 is a 28-year-old white female who was charged with a class 4 felony sexual abuse on a child. She sexually and physically assaulted her preschool age children over a two-year span. She has four children, three boys and one girl. Her identical twin boys are the oldest and her third son was born when they were two years old. Her daughter was born one year later. She had all four children by the time she was nineteen years old. She separated from her husband when she was 21 years old and has been divorced for two years.

Offender #3 is a 48-year-old white male. He had an incestuous relationship with his two daughters when they were 16 years old. He had been married for approximately 14 years before his wife refused to continue any type of sexual relationship with him. He then started to sexually molest his 16-year-old daughter for about 1 1/2 years. After she left home he began to sexually molest his younger daughter when she turned 16.

Offender #4 is a 34-year-old white female. She is married and has three children, two girls 14 and 15 years old and a boy who is 12. She began to fondle and perform oral sex on her son when he was eight years old and continued to do this for two years. She denied ever sexually touching her daughters.

Offender #5 is a 51-year-old white male. He was married one time from 1975 to 1982. He served 20 years in the military. After leaving the military he started to sexually molest prepubescent boys. He would carry on this abusive relationship with each of his victims for about two years.

Offender #6 is a 26-year-old white female. She sexually assaulted a 14-year-old boy when she was 24 years old. She was married for seven years and has three children; a four-month-old boy, a one-year-old girl, and a four-year-old boy. She acknowledged that she had two other victims, a 14-year-old female and a 17-year-old male. She said the only sexual contact she had with the 14-year-old female was kissing at a few parties she had at her house. The 17-year-old male, Jeff, was an old friend she dated for about eight months prior to meeting the victim of record.

Offender #7 is a 40-year-old white female. She is married and has three children of her own and three stepchildren. She participated in the sexual abuse of her 16-year-old stepdaughter who was the biological daughter of her husband. She and her husband were also involved in the manufacture and distribution of methamphetamines.

Offender #8 is a 30-year-old single white male. He has admitted to molesting approximately 30 prepubescent boys. He had a variety of occupations working with children which gave him ample opportunity to molest them, including being a house parent for an orphanage of young boys.

Offender #1

Introduction

Offender #1 is a 56-year-old white male. He has been married three times and has five children, three boys and two girls ranging in age from 21 to 31 years old. He is currently married to his third wife of one year.

At the time of his interview he was serving a sentence for sexually molesting a ten-year-old girl. This is his second time in prison for sexual assault. Sixteen years earlier he served 18 months for attempted sexual assault and indecent exposure on a nine-year-old girl. In addition to these two offenses, he stated that while he was a grade-school teacher for about 10 years he had molested 48 of his fourth-grade female students. He was never charged for any of the 48 offenses and the victims never reported the abuse.

The Interview

Recognizing his attraction to prepubescent girls

"I first realized I was attracted to young girls when I was 16. I started coaching youth sports with the idea it was just a summer job, a way to make money to put gas in the car. But I found out when I started coaching I was attracted to the 11- to 12-year-old girls. I was doing baseball. I was swimming. I was doing tennis, and then just a whole bunch of stuff. And it continued on through the year. When I wasn't playing sports myself I was working for Park & Recreation coaching. And I was too young at that point, or too scared, to move on any of these girls. But I was fantasizing to them. I mean, I've been, I've been masturbating since I was about 11 or 12. But, after I started coaching I was masturbating to the girls I was coaching, even though there was no assault there.

"I found that I am most attracted to 9- to 10-year-old females' blond, tall, blue-eyed, prepubescent, or just starting puberty. I look for girls who come from one-parent homes or for girls that don't have anybody to speak for them, or don't have anybody who would be there to listen to if they did speak. I look for people in low socio-economic situations and people that might be afraid of the police. My first victims when I was teaching were almost all migrant girls, kids of migrant farm workers. Because, you know, they're here one week, gone the next, you never see them again."

Why there were sixteen years between offenses

"This one I'm in here for now is the first one in 16 years. I was out there 16 years and I was okay; I had the pool of 12 and under girls around me that I would fantasize to, but I didn't even try to assault any of them. When I was arrested, the DA tried for a week in the newspaper, and on TV, they went back through all the old rosters, even the boys rosters, calling them all, finding out if I had ever touched any of them. And I didn't. They didn't have any more victims to pull in. And I told myself in those 15-16 years that I had it under control, but I knew…I knew the urge was there.

"The reason I stopped molesting was because I got arrested. I was arrested for attempted sexual assault on a nine-year-old girl. I tried to coerce her into my car in Denver; she was on the street alone. She got scared, and ran off, and I got caught. I plead guilty to attempted sexual assault, got three years, and did 18 months. I got out in '84, killed my parole in '85; and was fine until '98."

The grooming and setup of the victim of record

"I'm here for sexual assault on a child in a position of trust. She was a daughter of an acquaintance. She was 10 when we started, 11 when we stopped, or when I was arrested. I was in a position where I was given time alone with her. The mother, I think, saw me as a family friend because that was the image I put out there. I met them at a bar in May 1998 that I used to go to on Friday nights with about 15 to 20 of my friends and family for a couple beers, play some darts, and this kind of stuff. The mother was a barmaid at the bar. She latched onto us fairly quickly because we had a large number of people, and we all tipped well, and we're a pretty mellow bunch.

"It was my family, my son and his wife, my wife — or my future wife, a couple of buddies and their wives, people we worked with, customers from work. Everybody in our circles knew that we did FAC, which was Friday Afternoon Club, every Friday because nobody worked on Saturdays.

"We would drink, and some nights we would stay there and have a burger and fries or something. But we were usually gone by 8:00 pm.

"About the second Friday she had brought her daughter to work with her. After a while I asked her, who's the kid sitting over there in the corner? And she said, oh that's my daughter. Well, why did you bring her to the bar? Well, I couldn't afford a babysitter, couldn't find one, whatever, you know. So, somebody, I don't think it was me, but somebody said, well bring her over. Because they have a separate room with the dartboards in it where you could go back there and sit. Bring her back here with us and we'll talk to her, and keep an eye on her, and let her play darts with us or whatever. So she brought her back and every time her mom took a break, she sat with us and got involved in our group. Now when I first met the mom my first inclination was to try to ply her with money. My first impression of her was that she was someone who would do anything. I thought she probably had habits that she needed money to keep going. I thought drugs for sure, and watching her at the bar for a couple of weeks she drank like a fish too. I mean, she'd put away more beer working than we did just kicking back.

"The girl's name is April[7], that's better than saying 'the girl.' April had a younger half-brother that was in and out of the house with them. And finally the boy's father took him out for good. I wasn't sure what Mom's marital status was; all I knew was she had a continuing round of boyfriends. I met her in June 1998 and began molesting her around September or October the same year.

"My first thought. I figured she was single, whatever. You know, she was playing up to the guys at the bar. She was 30 years old or

---

[7] April is a pseudonym to protect the identity of the victim.

something, a good-looking lady. So I thought this might, this might be something. Because I was single and basically out of control sexually. At the time I was just using pornography tapes, for sexual relief. However, I had surrounded myself with a bunch of 12-year-old and younger girls, because I coached girls' softball. Even though none of them were ever victims, they were all part of my fantasy pool. So that was the situation I was in when I met momma. Well then when April showed up a couple weeks later, it appeared to me that she was playing up to all the males and ignoring the females. The other guys were polite to her but I on the other hand immediately became interested. She sat over by me and we had a great long conversation about everything, school and, you know, whatever. I then brought the mother into our circle. Basically at that point I started off trying to groom her, the mother, but also the daughter by now too. As time went on we got more involved together. She was in our circle, kind of thing. On her days off we'd go over to her house after work. They lived in assisted housing. It was an open invitation. We're going to barbecue tonight, if you want to and you've got time, come on down. And we'd barbecue, and drink beer, or whatever. They got involved that way and I wound up spending more and more time with April and less time with the adults when these parties were going on.

"She'd want to go out back and climb. She loved to climb. Once she got up on the roof and couldn't get back down. So I went out and got her down. We started to spend more and more time together.

"I found out some things from the mother's friends I hadn't known before. One of the things I learned was that April had been sexually abused by her father, who her mother had divorced. This new information increased the vulnerability, in my mind, of both of them. They're both very vulnerable to being manipulated and used because of the position they put themselves in. Not so much April, but with mom's drug and alcohol abuse. I found out from her friends that she'd been in and out of rehab. Social Services had been called on them two or three times, and I found out that April had been suspended from school twice for attacking teachers. At one point she threw an aquarium out the window of her classroom. As it turned out, one of my softball player's mothers was her teacher, and she was a good friend of mine. I mentioned that I knew April and they asked me if I could help her out with some of these grades and things, being an ex-teacher.

April's mother asked me if I would go talk to the teacher and see if there was anything we should be doing to help April. So I went and talked to the teacher, and she told me that the kid was showing up to school four days in a row in the same clothes. There would be two or three days there in a row where the only meal she was getting was the meal served at school. The school had called Social Services two or three times. This information again, fed into my little vulnerability thing, that if I attempt to assault April and April tells momma, you know, what's momma going to do? I know she's using cocaine; I know she's an alcoholic. Social Services is already looking at them. Everybody knew this information but I'm the only one that used it this way. I felt she was a safe target.

"I started to help her with her schoolwork, and working on science projects and this kind of stuff. I set it up to where it looks better than it is because they were calling me. Saying, what are you doing? Do you have time? She's got a science project or something she needs help with, can you come over? I would be like, well I've got to do this and this, and maybe I, well maybe I can squeeze an hour in here somewhere. You know, I made it sound like it's a big deal but I really didn't have anything to do. When they asked me to come over I was thinking, oh yeah, I'll get over there right now. I was trying to take it slow because I didn't want to get real crazy with it. So I would go and we would work on the schoolwork and mom and I would have a couple beers. Then I'd go home and that was the end of it.

"Then they started coming over to my house for barbecues. It got to the point where every time they came over she was always trailing me around. I was touching her in a nonsexual way. I would pat her on the back; put my hand on her shoulder or something. Basically what I was doing was getting her used to my touch, getting her used to being touched by me, having my hand on her. This went on for a while, and it appeared harmless so nobody made any mention of it.

"The first time I actually assaulted her was at the end of May. She called me at work and said that she had gotten an 'A' on some kind of school project. I don't know if it was a science project, or an end-of-the-year test or something, and could we go do something? I said, well yeah but I've got to work. I did have to work another couple of hours that day. I had stuff I was right in the middle of; I couldn't leave. I told her it's going to be a couple hours, but we can go get some ice cream or something. She said, no I want to go down to the river and feed the ducks. So I said, oh well, what does your mom say? Oh, mom doesn't care, you know. All this time in this buildup stage I was constantly slipping mom money for a power bill, electric, you know, whatever, the gas bill, I need to buy groceries or whatever. And my self-talk was, it was all going up her nose, and none of this going to April.

"Up until that point in time we hadn't been alone much. We'd just been alone for a couple minutes in the house, or a couple minutes out in the backyard, or whatever. We hadn't spent any real time alone. We'd maybe run over for an ice cream cone or something. Baskin-Robbins was five minutes away, get the cone, bring it back, and eat it out in the front yard kind of thing. I was giving her attention any time I could, that's what she was getting from me. It was a lot of little stuff. There were a couple days when it was raining hard when school was let out. Well, her mother's not going to come and pick her up, so I'd swing by and pick her up. Just little stuff like that, that as all grooming, it was all manipulating her. She was starved for affection of any kind at all, attention, and notice, whatever. She began to tell me things. I started initiating talk about sex.

"Well, I don't even know if it was actually sex to start with. I would ask her, you know, your mom is looking kind of rough this afternoon; did she have had a bad night or something? And she said, oh yeah, her boyfriend kept her awake all night, you know, whatever. They were down on the couch all night. I would ask her, 'well how did you know?' 'Well, they woke me up.' That would start the discussion about sex. Then she started telling me about what her dad did to her, and how she's got her little fourth grade boyfriend that she says she's giving oral sex to. I provoked the conversation to the point of keeping it going because this all went into my fantasy about her. I got aroused when we would talk like that, but that was all stuff that was going on for the first five weeks I knew her."

The sexual assault of the victim of record

"One afternoon I went to pick her up from a woman who lives two doors up from her. She was like a babysitter after school or whenever her momma wasn't there. She got in the car and we were headed up the street to go buy a loaf of bread and couple bottles of pop, and head for the river. Just as we were leaving, momma came screeching around the corner. Of course she needed $40 for whatever, which I didn't have on me. So I said, well, come on and follow me down to the bank and I'll get you something out of the ATM. Which I did, then she went her way and we went off our way down to the river.

"April was in a dress, the first time I'd ever seen her in a dress. And I immediately started formulating; okay we're going to go off alone here. I began immediately formulating plans about how I was going to fondle her today. Seeing her bare legs in a short dress was very arousing for me. Being in a short dress would make it easier to fondle her. It makes it easier to fondle genitals if there's just a dress in the way. We stopped, got our goodies and went down to the river and I tried to find a place along the river where I knew there were some trails that went back into the brush. I always carried a couple of folding chairs in the back for going to games, so you had a place to sit. I only grabbed one chair though with the idea that if she wants to sit, she's going to sit on my lap. There were two chairs there but I only took one because I was already planning ahead. We wandered down in through there, and there were a lot of bugs flying around. I had some bug spray, and we stopped and I said, let me spray some of this on. I sprayed it on her arms and legs. But then I had to rub it on a little bit, you know. She didn't say anything, she just stood there so I rubbed up to the hem of the dress and that's where I stopped. She just stood there, you know.

"I wanted to see what she was going to do, you know. I wanted to see if she'd freak out and jump back, say 'what are you doing?' At which point I would have stopped, and that would have been the end of that. But based on the stories she's been telling me, I didn't think she would. We went down to the river; she took off her shoes and socks, and actually exposed herself while she was taking the shoes and socks off. I know she didn't intend to, but she did. Her panties were baggy kind of things, which aroused me even more. I sat in the chair, and drank my pop, and watched her break up the bread and feed the ducks. She wandered around in the river a little bit. When she came back up, she crawled up on my lap and started drinking her pop. So we're sitting there and I'm rubbing her legs like from the ankles to the knees. I hadn't gone above the knees. She was just sitting there talking about the ducks and talking about school, and talking about whatever assignment it was that she got a good grade on. Then she put the bottle down and she laid forward on her legs because there was a spider or something down here on the grass that she had a blade of grass and she was playing with. When she did that I started rubbing her legs above the knee, and I asked her if she liked it, and she said, yeah it feels good. She asked me about the spider or something, did I think it was going to bite her or whatever? I said, I don't think so but I wouldn't get too friendly with it. I rubbed higher on her legs, got up to her panty line on her legs, and asked her if it still felt good? She said, yeah, and I asked her, would you like to have your back rubbed? And she said, yeah. So I started rubbing her back, outside the dress. But of course, I was pulling it up more all the time. She sat up and pulled the dress up and laid back down again and said, now the dress is making my back sore, so do it inside the dress. So I was rubbing her bare back while pulling the dress up, of course, which exposed her underwear. I was rubbing her back with one hand, and I put the other hand up inside her panties and was rubbing her vagina and rubbing her bottom, asking her if she liked it. She said, yeah my dad used to do that. You know, and I'm rubbing it and everything. And, you know, she's cool. She's talking about the spider, and she said, don't put your finger inside me because it will hurt. I said, okay so I just went ahead and fondled her. And after about 5 minutes of this, 10 minutes, I picked her up off my lap and put her on the ground and said, I need to go over here and go to the bathroom. So I went in some bushes and proceeded to masturbate. I looked around and she's standing back there watching me. So I turned my back to her, and she moved around where she could see it again. I asked her, do you know what I'm doing? And she says, yeah, my dad taught me how to do that. I said, well come over here and show me what you know. And she did. And that's where it all started right there.

"It continued practically every weekend, from the first of June until the first week in October of '98. And it steadily progressed. I would have her alone for a couple hours one day every weekend. We'd go out in the afternoon. Some weekends I had to pass because I had work going on or other things going on. All the times that we were alone we would do different things. Sometimes we would go driving or if she wanted to go rock climbing, horseback riding, or whatever, that was fine with me. When we were driving she'd sit on my lap and steer, and I'd work the pedals. All the time we were driving I was fondling her. This went on until October. One time I took her swimming to the hot springs where suits are optional. We both went into the men's room. We went in there and I stripped off, you know and she was standing there looking at me. I said, what? You know, you've seen it before. Then she stripped off. It was the first time I had ever seen her naked. She got in her swimsuit and then we got in the pool. We were the only ones in suits. I got out of mine as soon as I could. Eventually, after maybe 30 minutes or 45 minutes, I talked her out of her suit. So she was in the pool with me naked and I mean, there were other adults around, but I was just enjoying the power and control over her.

"Like I said, this went on until October, then one night they just up and moved out in the middle of the night. I did take pictures of her and performed oral sex on her two times. She never performed oral sex on me, I wanted her to but she wouldn't. There was never any penetration on my part because she was just scared to death of being hurt."

His description and perception of the victim of record

"I thought of her as being very precocious, that she knew what was going on, she knew about sex, she knew how to use her body to work men for money, to get what she wanted out of a man. She knew about oral sex; she knew about digital penetration; she knew about masturbation. She knew about porn movies. We did watch porn movies together. And she would talk about I don't want to do this or that until I'm older.

"After she left I tried to use the pictures I took of her to masturbate but it didn't work very well. I seem...it seems like I need, I need the contact. I need the closeness. I need to know the personality of the victim. I need to have an understanding of where they've been and how they're going to, you know, how I think they're going to react. I can't touch the pictures. They're not the same.

"The way I saw it with her I had three choices. It was like playing Let's Make a Deal, you've got Door 1, Door 2 or Door 3. Door 1 was just break off all contact and get the hell out of Dodge and don't go back, you know. This would have been the best thing for me but wouldn't have helped the kid. The second door was, go to Social Services, tell them what you think is going on, the neglect of the mother and all. And door #3 was to take advantage of a real vulnerable situation and use it for my advantage, which is what I did."

The abuse of his fourth-grade students

"One month after I got married the first time I fondled one of the girls in my class who came up to ask me a question or something. She was there at the desk, wearing a dress, and I began to rub the back of her thighs. I was talking to her, I said, does that feel good? Well, she said yeah it did, and I was about half-way up and I said, well I can stop there or I can keep on going; it's your choice. She said, no you can go on. So I went on higher, and I finally went and got all the way up to her genitals. That was it. That was the first time I molested one of my students. Before that I had molested my cousin when I was 11 and when I was between my freshman and sophomore years in college I fondled a six- or seven-year-old girl that was attending the day school where I was working over the summer. Then, after that it was, I was either 22 or just turned 23 when I assaulted my first student. The second year in the same location, I probably fondled every girl in the class. The longer it went the more I needed to do to get the rush. It's like when I was a kid I could steal a quarter from my Dad and that was cool. But now I'm an adult, picking off a quarter from somewhere, it doesn't have the same rush it had when I was a kid. The first student I assaulted, like I said, I fondled her underneath her dress. I did put my hand inside her underwear, and fondled her genitals. Nothing was said, it happened one time, and that was it. The following year I started doing that again. I think the next year was the first time I groomed, I started grooming everybody, all the kids in the class, everybody. I had my good person on. Everybody thought I was great guy. I had just gotten married, and when I wasn't assaulting, when I wasn't, you know, being deviant, I was a darn good teacher. I don't know what it was that made me a good teacher. Maybe it was because I was trying to put on a good image of being a good person, or maybe it was because I really did enjoy it. It might have a lot to do with the power and control thing.

"I would groom the whole class, boys included. They all thought I was a great guy. I care about them. I'll sit down and talk to them. I mean, really talk to them and find out what's going on. I would ask them how are things at home, are you getting enough to eat, this kind of stuff. If they come to me with a problem, I'll stop eating my lunch, give up my lunch hour, and go talk to them. Then after I had them all groomed, or while I was grooming them, I'd be picking out the ones that might be vulnerable. By acting like I was interested in them, cared about them, got me information about who's living with grandma that's blind, and deaf, who's living on Welfare or whatever. Who is the only kid in the house? Which one is a single child, because sometimes sisters will talk or, brothers and sisters will talk. If I had a single child living in a home with a single parent, who was like on the dole and spending it on beer. Or, a single parent whose working three jobs trying to get the bills met, then this kid didn't get much time at home. I knew the kid was vulnerable. I would single out kids that were being ignored. If they're working at their desk, and they're sitting there, and they're bent over working, and a key on a chain falls out from around their neck, I'll ask them, what's that to? Do you have a safe deposit box with a million dollars in it? The kid might tell me, 'Oh, that's my front door key, my mom doesn't get home until 6:00.' Right away, I would file that away. Some of that stuff is in their school records anyway. Single parent, momma works here until 5:00. If you need to reach her, you've got to call here because there's nobody home kind of thing. If I had a class of 30 kids, they all get groomed; they all think I'm a great guy. But, maybe I've got a group of 5 or 6 over here that I think are vulnerable that I'm also grooming even more than these other 25. Once I get them ready to follow me into the fire, then I just have to sit back and wait for an opportunity to come up. And it does, you know.

"The kids all trusted me. They were all…I mean, these are all fourth graders, so they're like nine-ten years old. I always told people I thought fourth grade was the best age because they're old enough to not have to have you tie their shoes for them all the time, but they're young enough that they haven't learned to be sarcastic. They're still gullible enough that I could reel them in. It would be things like…when they'd come up with skinned knees or whatever, you know, skinned elbows. I was always very tender with them, always concerned about them and never hurt them. This is one reason I think I got away with it for so long because I never hurt them. I never caused them physical pain. Psychologically, emotionally, you know. I've never had intercourse with a minor. There were two occasions where I tried, and I couldn't maintain the erection for whatever reason. And I know that both of these girls were in the process of being assaulted at home on a regular basis, which is why I figured they were fair game, because they can't do anything about it, you know. But I couldn't, I couldn't maintain the erection. I penetrated them digitally, but as far as intercourse goes, I couldn't do it for whatever reason. I tried.

"Everyone at the school trusted me and thought I was a great guy. I think everybody that is in any kind of a predatory mode is going to put out a socially acceptable aura about them. The great fallacy that sex offenders are hiding in bushes and lurking in trees and this kind of stuff is a crock. Because we're the guy who lives next door. We're the guy that's coaching your kid's baseball team, we're the priest at the church. Mentally, if we're working like we should, even though we're being deviant, we all want to put out that front that says, this is a nice guy. This is, you know, this is a good guy and he wouldn't do this kind of thing. And I do that by volunteering, working in the church. I was named Director of Summer Recreation down there at the end of that second year.

"My first victim as a teacher was an Anglo kid. She was not from a single-parent home, but her dad was an over-the-road trucker and he was never home. The second year I started out with the migrant kids because they were more vulnerable. This one migrant kid I groomed, I think she was 10, would follow me around when I'm doing duty on the playground. She'd want to stay in and clean the boards for me or whatever. At one point I caught her stealing money out of my desk. I thought, well, you know, we've got one here. This girl's going to do what I want her to do. When I caught her I told her we could do one of four things, which is call the cops and have them take you away; or, we can go to the principal and let him deal with you. All the kids in the school knew that he only had one way to deal with anything; he had a paddle about this long. Or, we can get in my car and we'll go over and confront your mother at work in front of all the people she works with and tell them that you've been stealing money and let you explain yourself. Well, of course, none of those options are cool. And then a fourth option is, well you and I can go downstairs in the locker room and deal with this ourselves and it will be over with. This is what she chose to do.

"We got down there and I said, okay, now you've chosen this option. If you and I are going to deal with it right now, then this is what we're going to do. I told her, the first thing to do is take off your clothes. And, you know, she didn't like that. I said, okay then let's go talk to your mom. Well, she didn't want to do that either so she took off her clothes. I fondled her and she masturbated me, and I penetrated her digitally. That was it. I said, all right, get your clothes back on, go back upstairs, put the money back in the drawer, and go outside.

"With other students I used different things. If you've got a kid that's struggling I would tell them, I know you're working hard on this stuff, but you're not getting it done. If you don't pick this up, you're not going to pass. Well that immediately freaked them out because you've got a parent who is just, you know, the kid is a walking billboard for the parent. The parent just can't have this; this will not be acceptable. That especially worked on kids that I thought were maybe being physically abused at home too. Daddy's got a short fuse; don't be telling Daddy you're not going to pass, because he'll slap the kid around. Well, the kid will do just about anything to avoid that."

How he started to relate sex to power and control

"It started off with my first little girlfriend, who is not a victim, but it's the first time I was exposed to sexuality. We started doing the things that we saw the adults doing in her daddy's pornography magazine. Because when I first saw the porno magazines that her dad had, they were male-female adults that showed intercourse, showed anal intercourse, showed oral sex, showed everything. My girlfriend and I were both six years old and we started off pretty much as even partners on this, we both knew nothing; we were as blank as that wall. We started to act out what we saw in the magazines, the magazines always showed the woman in the subservient position, the man is always on top. The woman is on the bottom, or on her hands and knees. The man was always in control. We were together like for three years before we moved back to Colorado. By the time the three years was up, she would just automatically assume the subservient position. I mean, we weren't actually having intercourse, but there was digital penetration, and oral sex, and this kind of stuff. I think that's where a lot of my power and control stuff started to come from, that I'm more powerful than the females are. As I got older and didn't have the self-confidence to approach girls my own age through high school, I began looking for girls I could be in control of. Girls my own age wouldn't let me do that; I couldn't manipulate them, I wasn't good enough at it, you know, to manipulate them. But I could manipulate, as I got older, grade school girls."

How he rationalized his abusive behavior

"Well, with the victim of record my justification leading up to it, was she's done it before, she knows what's going on, I'm not hurting her. Sometimes I would use a little physical pressure, and she'd finally just give up and let me do what I wanted. I got to the point where I'm saying, momma knows what's going on, momma's pimping out her daughter, as long as momma gets paid and the daughter gets to do what she wants to do and nobody gets hurt, then everything is fine. That was my justification for continuing. After we were done every time I would tell myself, oh I've got to cut this out. I felt scared. Like, she's going to go right home and tell. And I kept telling myself, momma can't tell anybody, momma's a coke addict, what's she going to do?

"As far as the students I molested, it's the same thing, they're getting something and I'm getting something. See, basically the same way I rationalize with April because with her it was like I was paying for a 10-year-old hooker. It was a 10-year-old prostitute. And, she thought...and see this is the same with the other kids, I'm sure, felt too, that this was a one-for-one deal. April wanted to go roller skating. Okay, so we would go roller skating for a couple hours. Then we leave and go driving around, I would get an erection and eventually she's on my lap driving. She knows it, she's wiggling around, laughing, you know, carrying on. I'm fondling her through her clothes. I've got one hand under her shirt and one hand between her legs, she's wearing shorts. We would stop somewhere, she'll masturbate me until I ejaculate, and then we'll go on. She thought it was a one-for-one deal.

"The other ones, the students, they thought it was a one-for-one deal. I'm going to get an 'A' on this test, which I would normally flunk; or I got out of having to study for it because I'm going to get the 'A' if I do this. Once they've done it one time, and there's no pain involved, they realize it only takes five minutes rather than study for an hour. It's an even one-for-one break."

How he manipulated victims to feel responsible

"There was a victim when I was teaching that I had primed to use her body to pass the class. She was a fourth grader. We had talked about it a couple times, but nothing happened. I was the one that was going to decide when we were going to do this, because I would push her into it eventually. I let her think that it was her decision. I told her that when she decided that she was done knocking herself out studying and still not passing, and she wanted to go the other way, she should let me know. Then one day there was a spelling test, and she missed everything. We sat down, and I said to her that I knew she took her book home to study for the test today. I asked her, did you study when you got home? No sir. What did you do? I went outside and played. Okay, then what did you do? Then I ate dinner. Okay, then what did you do? I watched TV and I went to bed. So, you had the book there but you didn't study at all, why not? Well because I wanted to use my body, sir.

"She was boxed into this corner here. I said, okay. So we went up to the library, which is vacant most of the time. I gave her a choice of using oral sex, anal sex, or vaginal sex. She chose oral sex. I had her undress me partially, and she took care of it, and that was the end of it. She got a good grade on the test and off we went. I told her at that point, I said, well that was fine; next time you've got to choose one of the other two. And next time never showed up because it was toward the end of the year.

"Then the following year they changed my class. She was back in my class again, but she was moving. She was only going to be there for a week. The school was so big they had to rent a church hall across the road for a classroom which is where I had my classroom. One day I sent everybody but her out for recess. I told her that she really didn't do much for me last year and I passed her anyway. I basically told her she owed me and by the time we finished talking I had conned her into performing oral sex on me. I fondled her. And that was the end of it; she moved at the end of the week."

Why he believes his victims did not report the abuse

"I think because, for the most part I was very careful. I had a great image with the people wherever I was. They all thought I was just a great guy. I didn't hurt them. I didn't abuse them physically at all. There were some victims I penetrated vaginally with my finger but only if the hymen had already been broken. I wasn't going to force it. I was very careful about picking victims that were vulnerable. They had nowhere to go with it. Even if they did tell, who would believe them over a teacher who everyone thinks is a great guy. And there was never any physical evidence."

Assault on a nine-year-old girl he picked up off the street

"I never had to shift the blame because I never got caught for assaulting any of my students. The only time somebody tries to shift the blame is when they get caught. As long as they get away with it, they're cool. Now I got caught in '83 and at that point I was just denying everything. I tried to minimize it. I told them that all I wanted to do was touch her. It was kind of a relief to get caught. I mean, when I got done assaulting someone, I almost got physically sick to my stomach. I worried about it. I was scared, and I kept telling myself, I'm going to give this up. But as time went on, it didn't go away. I just kept doing it over and over again; it didn't go away. I thought about what this was going to do to my family even though I never got caught at it.

"Then in '83 when I got caught it was like getting thrown in detox or something. You know you're doing stuff that is dangerous that you shouldn't be doing, and it finally catches up with you. It's like a great relief that now everybody knows and you can quit hiding now. I was still out on the street when the cops rounded me up. They just took me to the jail and sat me down, and then wanted to know what was going on. They were tag-teaming me basically. I mean, one guy was in there for like an hour. Then the other guy was in there for an hour. I finally just said, look you know, if I'd have got her in the car, I'd have touched her. That's what they wanted to know. You see, that's what I told them then. Again, I'm trying to minimize it because this is the first time I ever got caught but it wasn't the first time I tried to pick somebody off the street.

"The first time I picked someone off the street I got away with it. I think she was about nine years old. She was out collecting cans. I got her in the car by asking her to help me look for a lost dog because I couldn't look for the dog and drive at the same time. We were driving around for a while looking. We went up an alley, and then around behind some buildings in a remote area. I said, oh what's that over there? When she looked, I grabbed her. I told her that if she just behaved herself the pain of having her hair pulled will be all that she would have to put up with. She asked me, she said, what are you going to do to me? I told her, I don't know yet. I told her to just start taking off her clothes. She had bib overalls on and some kind of ballerina stretch outfit underneath. She took the bibs off. When she was naked and again she asked me, what I was going to do? I said, I didn't know, and I was rubbing her and fondling her, and then I tried to digitally penetrate her. Of course, she was intact so I couldn't penetrate her, I didn't really want to hurt her. I rolled her over and penetrated her anally. Then I forced her to perform oral sex on me. Afterwards I told her to get dressed and I took her back within a couple blocks of where I picked her up, dropped her off, and off I went. I told her, just do as you're told and it will be all right, kind of thing. But I knew she was scared.

"It was the second time I tried to pick up a girl off the street that I got caught. I told the police I just wanted to touch her. But by the same token I had adhesive tape and Vaseline in the car in the glove compartment. So, that was not my intention at all; I stocked up before I went cruising.

"I let the first one go because I don't want to hurt them physically. I obviously don't have a whole lot of empathy for my victims or I wouldn't be victimizing them. But on the other hand, I don't want to hurt them physically. I don't want them to cry."

Why he took the risk to molest a stranger

"Well, I don't know. I had spent the two years previously, '81 and '82, subbing in Colorado Springs and working. I was working every day but had no victims. I was coaching high school girl's basketball. I didn't have any problems there. I mean, high school girls are too old for me; I don't get any rush out of it. I had signed a contract for what I thought was for teaching high school social studies, and coaching. I was trying to make an attempt to get away from the elementary school. So when I got there I was teaching fifth grade. Well, they found another high school social studies teacher, but they couldn't find a fifth grade teacher. Since my certificate is K-12 they switched me to fifth grade. I was disappointed about that. When I'm under a lot of stress and don't have a victim I can go to readily, I tend to go out and cruise. What I had done in the past is just get them to come over to the car and I'd flash them. For some reason, and I have no idea why at this point in time, instead of flashing her I talked to her about getting into the car.

"My problems are all wrapped up in power and control. My dad was real controlling, and I've tried to be him my whole life and I can't do it. He was emotionless. He deals with things in his own way, doesn't need help, the family is his responsibility, and it's his job. I've tried to do that my whole life and I can't do it. I'm just not that good. And when things don't go right, I don't have enough self-confidence in myself to say, no it's okay, I don't have to be able to do everything. It builds up and my life gets out of control, so I'm trying to find something I can control. I don't know precisely what was going on at that point in time, but the idea of controlling that nine-year-old just came to me, because I had her. I had her. She was in my control. I could have killed her, I could have, I could have raped, and sodomized her, and strangled her, and thrown her out of the car. But I wanted to exercise control. I didn't want to hurt her. I wanted to be in control without physically hurting. I didn't think about getting caught. It was a spur of the moment. It was like, do it, you know. Do it. Just grab her, do it, touch her, you know, whatever kind of thing. That's why when she asked me, what are you going to do to me? I said, I don't know. I really didn't know. Sometimes I just lose my fear of fear. All the things that stop us from acting out, like people being around, or, she's going to scream, I don't want to get caught. All those rational fears that keep us from doing things just go away."

His advice for police interrogations

"I think that bringing my family into it might have tipped me over. I'm assuming that the investigator would ask questions like have you ever had these kinds of allegations made against you before somewhere else? Why would she lie about it? If you're not getting anywhere, then you might have to go maybe talk to my mom or dad about anything in my history that might help you because you have to investigate these allegations. If there's a history of it, then we may have to go talk to your mom and dad and see if they are aware of you doing anything like this when you were younger that might have led to this kind of situation coming up.

"I have been trying to hide this from everybody my whole life. Everybody that knows me thinks I'm a great guy. They don't know my other side where I'm over here molesting this 10-year-old. And I don't want anybody to know that, most of all my mom and dad. I don't even want my parents to know about the allegations. It might not even be anything you're going to do, but on the other hand, just that fear, fear of exposure is something we all carry with us all the time. That's why I feel so much better about myself now. I don't have any secrets. I've given up all the victims. But until I gave up all this, fear of exposure was the worse thing that could happen.

"See, when I was arrested the first time, when I got out everybody knew, and I made sure everybody knew, even when I was coaching everybody knew. One of the guys that coached with me was a police detective. And it was on the records in the computer system. I said it happened; I'm not trying to hide it. I don't advertise it. But if somebody asks, I'll admit it and tell them I did 18 months. That's all well and good because that's out there, I'm not worried about that. I was what I appeared to be, an outgoing volunteer coach, nice guy. Yeah, at home, at night, lying in bed by myself I might be masturbating to thoughts of my catcher, you know, and what she would look like naked, and how it would feel to touch her, or have sex with her, or whatever. But I wasn't doing that. I was talking myself out of it. When April came along, it was just too available, it was just too easy. I would have had to work hard to get up close to one of my softball players in a position to where I'm going to be with her a great deal of time alone. I'm going to have to work out a way to explain that, and I couldn't. With April, her mother made the explanation for me."

Offender #2

Introduction

Offender #2 is a 28-year-old white female who was charged with a class 4 felony sexual abuse on a child. She sexually assaulted her pre-school age children over a two-year span. She has four children, three boys and one girl. Her identical twin boys are the oldest and her third son was born when they were two years old. Her daughter was born one year later. She had all four children by the time she was 19 years old. She separated from her husband when she was 21 years old and has been divorced now for two years. She was arrested in February 1996.

The Interview

The abuse of the twins

"I was 18 years old when I started to abuse my kids. At first it was just violent. The first thing I remember doing is slapping one of the twins. Eventually this progressed to physical and sexual assault in where I was pinching and pulling on the twin's genitals. When they were about three years old I started to masturbate them. I didn't just focus abuse just on their genitals. I hit them across the face, on their butt, and I backhanded them in the chest; I've done damn-near everything that I had done to me when I was a kid. My dad used to physically abuse me. I never broke any of my kid's bones, or punched them with a closed fist. I think I pulled my punches, for sure. I smacked them a lot, but always with an open hand. I didn't want to break anything, you know. I didn't want to break their bones.

"Sometimes I hit them because they were doing something wrong, but most of the time it was just because I was angry. When I was knowingly being abusive to them it was always because I was angry. There were some times where they were doing something wrong and I would swat them on the butt, and they'd get one swat and it would be for something specific. But most of the time when I would abuse their genitals it was just because I was mad, it wasn't to correct something they did. I was just pissed off. I felt pulling and pinching their genitals would hurt them more than just slapping them. I still think that's much more hurtful.

"I've kind of run an awful lot of events together. It's hard to remember all that I did. An awful lot of what I was doing is kind of mixed up and jumbled in my head so the timeframes are hard for me to keep straight. I know that things got progressively worse. Things went from physical abuse to sexual abuse and throughout there was verbal abuse. I don't know how much of it they understood at that point in time. I still don't know how much they understand.

"In my opinion, I physically and sexually abused all four children but I don't think that I could lawfully be charged with my daughter. I never physically abused her but when I would breastfeed her I think it was probably just the way I felt when I was breast-feeding her. I know some of that is normal biological, but I'm not clear about some things. I'm not sure if it was sexually gratifying or not.

"With the twins things progressed over time. I went from slapping and hitting them to pinching and pulling and being physically abusive with their genitals. Then I went from that to masturbating them when they turned three. This only happened with the twins and that was the progression over time. With my middle child, things started with him when I had my daughter. He was about one and he was walking and when I was breast-feeding my daughter and he would come and try to touch my breast. I would smack him. I was usually fairly calm and peaceful when I was breast-feeding and he would try and come and encroach on that. I would hit him for that. Then I got to the point where I would invite him to touch my breast and I would hit him. Not when I was breast-feeding but at other times. It was uh…um, I'm not even sure. I would usually be stewing about something when I would invite him to touch my breast. I was angry a lot. I would be sitting down somewhere and I'd have him come to me. He'd sit with me, and he'd turn around and touch my breast and I'd smack him. I would walk around the house in various states of dress and I would put myself out there, you know, knowing he would reach out to touch me."

Her arrest and interview with the police

"It all stopped shortly before my house burnt down. The twins just turned four. The abuse had been going on for about two years. I really went through this thinking process that I thought I was turning into my father. I could recognize the behavior and I decided I wasn't going to do that. I was tired of...I was tired all the way around. I was physically and sexually abusive to my kids. I was being physically and sexually abused by my husband. I was tired of the circle. I had nothing but violence most of my life, and I was tired of it, and I didn't want to continue to perpetuate that.

"The house burning down was an accident, it was a fluke, and it was nobody's fault. There was faulty wiring in the house and so, you know, it caught fire in the walls. When my house burnt down we were left homeless so we went to go stay with my mom. Now that I was staying with her I had other people there in the household which made it difficult to abuse them because I wasn't alone with them very often. The opportunity was gone, which definitely helped. Also, I had help now with taking care of my kids, which dramatically reduced the amount of stress that I was under. Added to that, my ex-husband was in jail at that point in time. All the way around my overall stress level, at least in some areas of life, was dramatically reduced, which helped. I actually ended up with quite a bit of help right after that in more ways than one. After a while we moved out into a place of our own. Things were pretty bad then.

"In March of '95 we were being evicted from the place that we were living in. It was horrible. My ex-husband was in jail, because he was a habitual traffic offender. He got arrested while he was going to pick up glass to replace all the windows that got busted out the night before from our domestic dispute. So he was in jail, we were getting evicted, and I was trying to bond my husband out of jail. My brother was baby-sitting my kids, and when I came home the police and Social Services were there. Social Services were removing my children, because of the unsafe environment. That's how my children ended up in foster care. It was while they were in foster care that the allegations of abuse were made. There was a length of time while they were in foster care that I was doing visitation and stuff, and so was my ex-husband. We were still together right at this point in time. I left him a couple months later and dropped out of sight. I quit visiting my children, because my ex-husband was stalking me and I was pretty fearful. Any time I showed up someplace he did things to my car. I'm not really sure how the allegations came out about me abusing my kids. The only thing I have to go on is what I was told. And according to the report that I was given, one of the twins made some basic disclosure, I guess, to their foster mother, or the present foster mother at the time.

"They did a videotaped interview of my kids and nothing was disclosed in the videotaped interview. But since a disclosure had already been made, I offered to go to the police department and speak with the investigators. They wanted to polygraph me, and against the advice of my lawyer, I said I would go take the polygraph. After the interview I was told that they would not polygraph me. They said I would not be a good candidate for the polygraph.

"They interviewed me about whether or not I had sexually or physically abused my children. And of course I denied everything. Well, then the court process started. I took a plea bargain. So I made an admission of guilt in court, under the law. But I didn't make a true admission of guilt until after I had been incarcerated.

"I didn't admit anything to the police because I didn't want to go to jail. I was pretty much in shock. I don't even remember a whole lot of my court hearings. I remember little things, but I was pretty numb and kind of in shock most of the time. When the police talked to me there was one detective and a polygrapher present. I had an attorney because I was going through a civil case but I agreed to talk to them without my attorney there. You see, whenever the Department of Social Services gets involved in a child being removed from the home you go through a civil matter. It's called a dependency and neglect petition. So I was undergoing that.

"I denied everything to them. I believe that speaking for myself, unless I am comfortable within myself and I can establish some sort of basic trust level myself, you know, a person has to be ready to come out of denial on their own. The same premise is true with treatment. You can't treat somebody who doesn't want to be treated. You can force-feed them any kind of philosophy and they don't have to take it, they don't have to utilize it."

How anger was the precipitator to abuse

"I'd say 90 percent of the time I was pissed off at my ex-husband for something. He would never let me out by myself. This created some serious, serious problems. He was a drug addict and an alcoholic. He was possessive, controlling, domineering; you know, if you ask my opinion, I married Satan.

"I think the twins endured the brunt of the abuse, probably just because they were the oldest. While I was abusing them I was always angry. I was always angry, raging. After I would abuse them I was still mad. I was angry a lot. I don't think the anger ever went away. And when I wasn't angry and started to feel bad about what I did, then I got mad because I felt bad. I would kick myself and then get angry because I was kicking myself. It turned into a vicious little cycle there.

"I felt bad about victimizing them. Because I knew I was victimizing them, and I knew exactly what kind of harm I was doing. And then I would be just appalled, and I would be angry at myself for doing it, and then I would just get mad, and then I would start the whole blame game again. I blamed everybody and everything for how rotten my life was. Everybody and everything. Sometimes I blamed them for even being born.

"They were only being children, you know. Kids get into things. They are curious, you know. I'd get mad when they made a mess, because they'd get into everything. The next thing I know they were climbing on top of the refrigerator, and I didn't know what to do. I was going six directions at once, and I didn't have any understanding or ability to cope. I had no parenting skills. I didn't know what to expect of them. I had no realistic expectation. And I blamed them just for being themselves. I didn't realize that their behavior was just being kids at the time.

"Why I focused my anger on their genitals, I couldn't tell you. I couldn't tell... I really couldn't tell you. I didn't get any sexual gratification out of it. I just knew it hurt them. And I knew that it would be a lasting hurt. I had some pretty lasting lessons myself. I learned through experiences the most effective way of hurting another individual. Besides sexually and physically abusing them, I would say really hateful mean things. You know, I hate you and wish you hadn't been born, it's your fault, things like that."

Her abusive childhood

"My dad started to physically abuse me when I was about three. I was physically abused by my dad until I was six. Then my parents got divorced and my father re-married. Then I was physically abused by both my dad and his new wife.

"I was hit with things, like belts, switches, and brooms. I've been hit on my butt, my back, my face. I went out of my way to take the majority of the punishments so that my younger brother wouldn't go through it. If he did something that was wrong, I would tell my dad that I did it. Or I could see my dad getting ready to hit my brother and I would get his attention.

"When I was seven I started being sexually abused by my baby-sitter's 14-year-old son. This went on for three years. I had no one to tell. My babysitter didn't know what her son was doing. And I most certainly couldn't say anything to my dad. She, my babysitter, happened to find me covered with bruises, and welts and cuts, and confronted my parents, and I just got beat worse for it. I got beat so bad that I couldn't move."

How she rationalized her abusive behavior

"I didn't really rationalize the abuse. What I did instead, and I do this an awful lot, I don't emotionally connect. So I take experiences, or memories, or even the possibility of a feeling and I shove it in a little box, and I put lots of tape and everything around it, and I put it out on a shelf. And rather than rationalizing it, I took it completely out of my head.

"I knew that it was something I shouldn't have done. I didn't make it okay with myself. I knew exactly what I was doing; I knew that what I was doing was wrong. And when I felt bad about it, I didn't feel any better about it. I couldn't make myself feel any better about it. Because I knew that the things I was doing were things that had been done to me. I knew what they were doing. I knew. I knew what the effect was. So I took it, I took it and I fed it into my anger. And I was going through not just a cycle of abusing my children, but I was going through a domestic violence cycle, I was going through… I was acting out my anger in a lot of different ways. And then when I got to feeling too bad about it, I took those real negative feelings, after feeding it into my beliefs about myself and the world around me, and then I took the remainder of it and I packaged it up and stuck it on a shelf in my head. And there are things that I can pull down at any point in time to say you know, I'm a really crappy human being."

Why she thinks people abuse children

"Lots of people go through physical abuse, sexual abuse, mental abuse, emotional abuse, and don't sexually assault. Lots of people. So none of those are reasons why people sexually assault. People do it out of an aggression. They do it out of a warped distorted way of thinking. And you can't crawl into somebody's mind. Sexual assault is out of power, it's out of control. I'm sure that sexual gratification can play somewhere into it, but that's not the reason for it. I never felt sexually gratified, or aroused or anything when I was abusing my kids. I did, however, have a sense of control and dominance that I didn't have with my ex-husband."

Offender #3

Introduction

Offender #3 is a 48-year-old white male. He had an incestuous relationship with his two daughters when they were 16 years old. He had been married for approximately 14 years before his wife refused to continue any type of sexual relationship with him. He then started to sexually molest his 16-year-old daughter for about 1 1/2 years. After she left home he began to sexually molest his younger daughter when she turned 16.

The Interview

The sexual abuse of his two teenage daughters

"I moved to Loveland in 1988, which is about the time my wife quit having sex with me. I thought for a while it was because of medical problems. She has had some female problems, some diabetes and a few other things. And for about three or four years I just thought that was the way it was because of her medical problems. Then I found out that she was having relations with other men. So I started to think about having sex with other women. I started fantasizing. When my oldest daughter turned 15, I started fantasizing about her. She was home all the time; she was involved in sports; I was involved with her, so we spent a lot of time together. It had been about five or six years since I had had sex with my wife. And one day I just, after fantasizing about my daughter for about four or five months, I just decided that my daughter would then take the place of my wife. I started out by fondling her and it progressed to having intercourse with her. This went on for about a year and a half. When she turned 17 she and I got into an argument about my molesting her, and she said that she didn't want to do it anymore, she didn't like it, and she didn't want me to touch her anymore. So I stopped. She never told anyone as far as I know and I thought that I had finished with that. Then about three to four years later my younger daughter turned 16, and I started the same process again, fantasizing about her, and then molesting her. That went on for approximately six months, and then I was confronted by the police, and arrested, and sent to prison."

His Marriage

"My wife and I were married for about 14 years before she started withholding sex from me. Up until then I thought we had a healthy, regular sexual relationship. I was in the service at the time. I was career service in the Navy. I spent about half of the time away from home, about six months out of every year on average I was gone. So I wasn't at home very much. When I was at home, I thought we had a good relationship. But I found out later that my wife had been an adulteress for years. When I finally reached the point where I retired, and came home and stayed home, she just decided at that time to stop having sex with me. And I, like I said, I believed that it was due to medical reasons. Because I knew she did have some problems.

"When I first moved back and I stayed at home, you know, I was expecting us to go on like we had during the sporadic times when I was home. I asked her, I said, is there a problem? Why don't you want to have sex with me? And she said, I just don't feel like it anymore. So that's one of the reasons that I thought that it was a medical problem.

"I worked in a place where there were a lot of women but I didn't think about having any kind of relationship with them. I went to work for a university, and there were a lot women that worked there; some of them were my bosses. I just maintained a social relationship. I had thought at one point of going out and maybe finding a woman to have a relationship with, but I never did.

"We talked about getting a divorce, but by the time that I had started fantasizing about my daughter, and I was very angry. I was angry because I wasn't having sex with my wife. I was angry because I'd found out that she was doing other things. We argued more than discussed anything. Every time divorce came up, she would say, sure go ahead, file for divorce, but you can keep the kids and everything else. So, you know, I just blew it off. I figured at some point it would, you know, take care of itself.

"Even though she said I could have a divorce and keep the kids, I didn't want a divorce because I also thought that it would be a sign of failure, that I wasn't able to maintain a household. My wife was doing things that would embarrass me. I lost control. So I isolated that part of my life and turned the rest of my life into being as normal as possible, even more outgoing. I became involved in youth sports and spent as much time as I could away from home. I spent more time at work. I would leave for work early and get there an hour before anybody else got there."

How fantasy developed into the sexual abuse

"Well, the fantasies actually started out about other women that I had known. Prior to my marriage, while I was in the service, I had contact with a lot of prostitutes overseas. I started fantasizing about the times that I had had overseas. There were times when we would go out and try to do as far-out a thing as you could find just to one-up each other while we were in the Service. I was doing tours in Vietnam so we didn't really care about what was going on. At that point I had no intention of marrying or anything.

"After I retired and my wife and I quit having sex, that's what my fantasies were based on, mostly these women I knew when I was in the service. Then about maybe a year or so before I started to molest my oldest daughter, I started including girls my daughter's age in the fantasies. At first I thought it was just, you know, spreading out my fantasies because they were starting to become stale to me.

"The girls I fantasized about, I left them a blank face because that was probably when I started fantasizing about my daughter, but I was still hiding it from myself. I had no physical attraction to any of my daughter's friends so I wasn't fantasizing about them. I knew a lot of them. Like I said, my daughter was involved in sports so I knew a lot of her friends but I had no attraction to any of them. Then, about four months or so before I actually molested my daughter the first time, I included her as the girl in my fantasies.

"The first time I molested her I was sitting downstairs and I had been fantasizing about her. I believe it was a weekend day because I was home during the day. I had been fantasizing the night before; I had fantasized most of the day. I called her downstairs and I had her sit in my lap, and then I started fondling her. I fondled her breast. She didn't say anything at first, but I could feel her tense up and stuff. And that was about as far as it went the first time.

"It wasn't uncommon for her to sit in my lap. I had always been real close with all my children like that. I spent so little time with them, that when I was home I always hugged them, all of them, all the time. I did this with both of my daughters and my son. I tried to be as close to them as I could whenever I was home. Because, like I said, sometimes I would be home for two or three days and I'd be gone for six months. I never saw this as grooming them for the molestation. That came about later. I know that, probably in the period before I actually molested her the first time that the hugs and stuff were becoming more often, leading up to the molestation. Usually I would be sitting watching TV or sometimes we would even be in public, like at a basketball game; she'd come and sit on my lap. Like I said, it was common for all of my kids, even my son up to a certain point, where he would sit in my lap.

"When I first fondled my daughter's breast she stiffened up. She didn't look at me. She just turned her head away. I fondled her outside of her clothing. I think she was wearing jeans and a t-shirt, with a bra underneath of it. Yeah, it was in, it was in the afternoon. I think she had just come in from outside or something. This went on for maybe five minutes, five to ten minutes at the most. I didn't say anything to her while

I did this. That pretty much became the routine for about a month or so. After that I put my hands inside of her clothing, underneath her bra, and fondled her breasts that way. Then I fondled her vagina outside of her clothing. I would do this for about, I don't know, maybe 20 minutes. This always occurred in the house somewhere; sometimes when we were downstairs watching TV in our den, sometimes we were in her bedroom, and sometimes we were in my bedroom.

"Most of the time when I would be fondling her, my wife was gone. She spent a great deal of time away from home. She had a job that she worked during the days. Most of the molestations, though, took place in the evening or at night. My wife would leave. She would come home from work and leave. She always had a different reason or an excuse, she was going with her sister to do something, or she was going to help a friend do this or do that. But she was gone quite a bit of the time. My son was older so he had a life. He was a senior in high school. And he pretty much was gone. He was getting ready to leave home and stuff. And my younger daughter was pretty much on her own. That was one of the things that later on caused me quite a bit of depression and stuff, was the fact that I look back and realize that I pushed her away at the time. I deliberately ignored her, or caused her to feel uneasy around me, so she wouldn't want to be around me. And I did that so that I didn't have to worry about her bothering me when I was molesting her sister. She usually stayed either in her room or upstairs somewhere. We had a split-level house.

"I never really said anything to my daughter while I was molesting her. It was pretty much just a physical thing. I know that she didn't want to say anything to me. And I didn't particularly want to have a conversation with her either. I was more interested in getting my wants met than I was talking with her about it. And I was embarrassed too, somewhat, and ashamed. So I didn't want her to put me in a position where I had to acknowledge what I was doing.

"Right after she would leave I would masturbate, and that would relieve me, and at the same time I got more angry at myself because of what I was doing. I got more angry at my wife because I was blaming her. I would say to myself, this is never going to happen again. And then it would go away for awhile. And then it would, I would start fantasizing again and building back up to that point again where I would molest her.

"Usually it would start after I came home. During the day I would keep myself busy at work, or doing something like if I was coaching a practice or a game, I would stay gone and I would keep myself occupied with those thoughts and try not to think about my daughter. Then I would come home and I would want to have sexual relations with someone. And every time I would say to myself, I'm going to confront my wife. We've got to do something about this. Then my wife would either not come home, or she'd call and say she wouldn't be home until late or something. I'd start to get angry and frustrated, and want to have something. And then my daughter would come home, and that would be all the impetus I needed to go ahead and start molesting her."

How fondling progressed to intercourse

"After, oh I don't know, maybe three or four months of, you know, fondling her, and then masturbating, I wanted more. So, I started having her fondle me. And then I would attempt to masturbate her; in my mind I was thinking that, if I got her excited, she wouldn't mind. Then I would have her masturbate me. That went on for a real short period of time, maybe only a couple weeks, where I would make her masturbate me, and then my trying to masturbate her.

"By this point I had already determined that my daughter was now my wife. She had taken the place of my wife. I gave her a lot more responsibilities in the house. I gave her the same control over her sister and brother that my wife would have had. I expected her to do things for me that I expected from my wife - cook my meals, be my companion, and enjoy the things that I enjoyed. I had put myself in that frame of mind; that's all I thought about. Within a couple of weeks I performed oral sex on her. That led to my forcing her to have oral sex with me. Then I would start to spend more time watching her and stuff. I would walk into her bedroom, as if she was, you know, my wife and that was expected. I started having her take showers with me. Every time we did that there would be molestation, either masturbation or oral sex. Then about, six to seven months after that I went into her room one night, had her undress, and I had intercourse with her. That then became what would happen. Whenever I would molest her from that point on, it would just be intercourse, with some foreplay. I would make her masturbate me, and or oral sex, and then completing with intercourse.

"It all started out as just sex to me, after a while though it was an obligation. I knew she was my wife at that point. And as my wife, I was obligated to have sex with her. I enjoyed the sex and it also filled my wants. The relationship wasn't based on the sex, but the sex was part of it.

One time, she came to me and said that she was going to tell her mother. I said, go ahead, she already knows. After that point, it was never brought up. It was like she had come to expect that that's how her life was. I was going to be coming in whenever I wanted and molest her."

How he used bargaining

"She was involved in soccer and she was very good at it. She won a scholarship because of her skills. It takes a little bit of money to do that. So I would pay for her to go to training camps, buy her special shoes, things like that. When she wanted a car, I went and got her one. I bought her clothes, makeup, whatever she needed. During the time I was molesting her I gave her financial rewards, more than I gave the other two children. I believe my older son knew what was going on, but I don't know for sure that he did."

His perception of his daughter's reaction to the abusive behavior

"My daughter never said that she liked it, enjoyed it, or anything like that. There were probably more than a few occasions where she would say 'no' but in a real hushed kind of scared way. You know, like a plea, but didn't really want to put it out there. Towards the end, up until the time that she confronted me, she was like, you know, from the time I would start molesting her until I left, it was probably like she put herself somewhere else. You know, her body was there but she wasn't. She didn't respond anytime that I know of, other than what physical responses, you know, a person would have. But, no, she never said she liked it or anything like that. I told myself that she liked it. That was one of the justifications I used to continue what I was doing. I told myself I was doing what she wanted. Otherwise, she would have said something."

How he felt about sexually abusing his daughters

"I felt guilty and ashamed about what I was doing. As time went on the feelings intensified. I identified them as anger, because they were more intense. By the time I was regularly having intercourse with her I was angry and fighting with my wife continuously. We didn't sleep in the same room anymore. We never talked to each other. Even though she made my meals for me we never ate our meals together."

What precipitated the abusive behavior

"Sometimes I would be told that my wife was seen at a party with another man, and that would lead to my molesting my daughter, probably within a day or so. If my wife and I got into a fight, it would lead to me molesting my daughter on a daily basis. If my wife left, for example, she would go somewhere on a trip with her sister I would molest my daughter on a daily basis. So sometimes there was a particular incident that might happen and sometimes it was just the opportunity was there.

"Drinking was never a reason I molested my daughters. I quit drinking when I was 34 years old. I just quit. I use to binge drink in the service, because being on a ship, you know, we were out at sea 45 to 110 days. You pull in somewhere and you're there for three days; you've got maybe one or two days off. It was our habit to drink as much as you could at that time. When I was 34 I received a shore duty tour of three years where I was an instructor. I was drinking as if I was going to be gone away from alcohol for 45 or 90 days, and I was drinking every day like that. It finally got to the point one night when I was very drunk, I blacked out, I didn't remember where I was. I forgot where I had parked my truck. I had called home several times to have my wife come and get me. But I was never there when she came to get me. I would leave or something. Then when I would finally get home, my son, who I think was eight at the time, would ask me, Dad, you're a drunk? That was the last time I ever drank."

Why he stopped sexually abusing his oldest daughter

"When my oldest daughter turned 17 she had a boyfriend. She was reaching the point where she was looking to leave home. Not because of what I was doing, but because that would have been a natural thing for her to do. At this point she was growing up; she was getting to be an adult. She was probably around more people that would discuss about kids being molested by their parents, relatives and other things like that. She probably felt bad that I was interfering with her relationship with her boyfriend, and maybe making her feel like she wasn't being faithful to him, something like that. And then she probably just decided that it, she wasn't going to have it anymore, that she didn't want me to continue molesting her. One day I went down into her room with the intention of molesting her again. And she said 'no!' I told her we're just going to do it or something, I'm not sure of the exact words. This wasn't the first time she said no, but she never said it that way. The other times that she had said 'no' were very few, but they were very suppressed; you know, kind of like with her face turned or something, and she would say 'no.' This time, though, she just sat there and said, 'No! I'm not going to!' And I started demanding that she take her clothes off, or that she let me hold her. She resisted. I grabbed her by her arms, and held her down, and she was crying. I think at that point it really hit me what I had been doing. I don't even remember a lot of the conversation. I was trying to make myself angry to the point where I didn't care. But then she started crying and she had a scared voice that I had never noticed before. That kind of shook me up pretty bad. So I left, and that was the last time I ever molested her."

The sexual abuse of his youngest daughter

"My younger daughter was about 13 years old when her older sister was 17. It was probably three years after I stopped molesting my oldest daughter that I started molesting her sister. She was about 16 years old when I started to molest her. During that three-year period between the molestation of my daughters I went through some depression that I internalized. I was really unhappy with myself. But I was becoming even more and more angry at my wife, at my relationship with her, and the situation that we were in. I started spending money, buying things that I didn't need, doing remodeling projects that were very expensive. You know, it helped the house but it really wasn't necessary. I had gotten into a debt, not a lot, but there was enough there that the amount of free money I had was dwindling.

"My oldest daughter stayed living in the house until she graduated from high school. She went away to college. My son had moved to Michigan. It was just me, my wife, and youngest daughter in the house at this time.

"During those three years between the abuse I had no sex at all, nothing. I didn't even masturbate during that time. I had said to myself if I couldn't have sex with my wife I wasn't going to have sex with anyone.

I wasn't going to hurt anybody again. Then two of my nieces told my mother they had been at a party with my wife. My nieces were about 17 or 18 at the time. My wife was about 45 or 46. She was at a party with one of their friends who was 17 or 18. They said she was using alcohol and drugs, and that she had left with this guy who was 17 or 18 years old. My first inclination was to confront my wife, but I was a little afraid to because I wanted to hurt her, and I wanted to hurt her very bad. I had even thought about killing her. And then I said, well, if she can do it, so can I. I knew that she had known that I had molested my older daughter. I said, well if she doesn't care, then I'll just continue on. And that's when I started to fantasize about my younger daughter. It followed the same pattern as with my older daughter. I called her downstairs, and when she came, sat on my lap, I fondled her breast. Then it followed almost exactly the same all the way up to the night that I had intercourse with her. But I never completed intercourse with either of my daughters. I always ended up with masturbation. Intercourse would last until I knew that I was reaching a point where I was going to go; I would stop with the intercourse and then masturbate.

"I molested my youngest daughter for about six months. As far as I knew she didn't know anything about me molesting her older sister. My two daughters never talked about it with each other. They didn't know that I had done anything to the other one. The only person that I knew for sure was aware of the abuse was my wife, and I believe my son knew. But my two daughters, I think that they were so ashamed of what I had done to them that they didn't want anybody to know. I don't believe that they knew that their mother knew, or accepted that she knew. My oldest daughter may have known her mother was aware of the abuse; I'm not sure. My wife and I never discussed the abuse. My wife and daughter's relationship became very strained. But I always had a good relationship with my oldest daughter. In fact, we even developed a better relationship after I stopped molesting her than we had before I was molesting her. Now I don't have any kind of relationship with either of my daughters because they're my victims. I'm not allowed to contact them. I've been told by others that they still have concern for me.

"After the first night that I had intercourse with her, she told a friend of hers the following day. Well, she didn't tell. What I understand from the statements was the friend noticed a change in her and she asked, you know, something going on at home? And my daughter, I guess, said yes. Her friend asked her, is your father doing something to you? And I guess she said, 'yes' or responded in some way that the girl felt that there was something going on. This girl told her mother, and that woman informed Social Services. They called the police. And then a police officer came to the house and questioned me that night."

His interview with the police

"The police questioned me for about an hour that night. I described any contact I had with my daughter as, you know, wrestling, regular contact. I told them there was never anything inappropriate. They were only questioning me about my younger daughter because my older daughter was living in Nebraska at the time. I didn't admit anything to the police or anybody else. The first time I admitted it was after I came to prison and started treatment.

"Then Social Services called and they asked if I would come in and talk to them. I had gotten a lawyer and he said 'go in and talk to them, but don't admit to anything.' I still had not been arrested.

"I had an attorney originally because my wife had started divorce proceedings. She started the proceedings because of the accusations. I even denied it to my attorney at first. But after the police came I went back and told him everything that was going on. I admitted to him that I had molested my two daughters. Then when Social Services called he said, just don't admit to anything, just go and talk to them and see what's going on; you know, see what's happening.

"I'm not sure when the charges were filed. It was a while later. I think they went and talked to my daughter in Nebraska. I'm thinking maybe it was maybe about a month later.

"When the police were talking to me I never even considered admitting anything to them. I didn't trust them. Part of my training in the service was what they call SEAR training, survival of asian rescue for POW training. And part of that training was being interrogated. So I knew that this person wasn't there for my benefit, he was there for his reasons, to find out what had happened. I knew that he would use various techniques, whatever he could think of to find out what happened.

"The detective showed concern for my feelings, my emotions. You know, telling me things like, you know, this is probably a burden, you really want to get rid of it, I know you do. And if you get it off your chest, you're going to feel a lot better. He said I should think about my daughters, what they're going through. He would then ask me questions and then going back over the same things again.

"I was trying to find a way out with the least amount of pain. So I was holding out to find out what my options were. I went to treatment before any kind of trial, and in treatment I told them that I had been accused of molesting my daughters, and that I had some other problems that went along with that. Then my lawyer came and told me that the District Attorney had made up a list of charges, and offered a plea agreement. So I said, okay I'll take the plea agreement. There were two charges of aggravated incest, one, I was given a sentence of 16 years; and the other one I was given a sentence of 4 years to lifetime supervision."

His advice for police interrogations

"I think the thing that probably would have caused me to come forward quicker is if I had been approached from the point of view that my daughters were suffering. Even though the detective said "Think of your daughters, think about how they feel." And at that point, I wasn't worried about how they felt. I felt that they were okay. He didn't say anything to make me think that they were suffering, that they were in pain. He didn't say anything like they were embarrassed to be around their friends, things like that. If it had been presented to me like that and if he said they were depressed, they were at the point of committing suicide, or they were really hurting themselves somehow, but they can't get any help unless I come forward. I think at that point I would have."

Shifting the blame and rationalizing the abusive behavior

"At the point when I was molesting my daughters I was blaming my wife and myself. My wife, because she stopped having sex with me and started having sex with everybody else. Myself, because I made the conscious decision to hurt my daughters rather than to confront my wife, or to seek outside help. And I blame both of us because we established a household where what we did was right. And so, those are the only ones I blame.

"What used to drive me was the lack of attention from my wife, or lack of companionship. If I'd have had that, I don't know that I would have thought about having sex with my daughters. To rationalize the abuse I used a lot of different things. I would tell myself they're going to have sex anyway. Strangers would hurt them; I won't. The boys in school don't really care about them and if they have sex, it's just going to be for their own gratification. I told myself they're going to like me for it. Eventually they're going to enjoy having the sex. Things like that. With my older daughter, I rationalized by telling myself that she knows her mother is being unfaithful to me, and not having sex with me. I used anything that I could think of that would put me in a better light with them in a relationship."

Why he began sexually abusing his daughters at the age of 16

"I waited until they were 16 years old because I don't have any sexual interest in underdeveloped children. And I think when they started acting like women, I started to treat them like women. My younger daughter had a medical problem that required special treatment at Children's Hospital. She was advancing, or her body was developing too fast and they had to hold her back. She was taking medicine for that. So I didn't, I never saw her as a sexual partner or anything until she was 16 and she pretty much had developed, and she looked a lot like her mother."

Why he did not molest anyone outside his family

"I had contact with lots of young girls. They didn't build any desire in me; they still don't. It was not only that they were my daughters, but they were my wife's daughters. If they hadn't been my daughters but they had been her daughters, I think I would have done it for the same reasons. The biggest part for me was because I wanted to have sex. But there was a driving part of it that was, when she knows, she's going to be hurt because she didn't protect her daughters. So a big part of this was to spite my wife. Also, I was still being the man of the house. I was still, you know, the husband. I was still getting what every husband is supposed to get. At least that's what I thought.

"Of course, there's always a chance that even if things had changed a little bit, there's a possibility that it could have happened. I think the risk would have been a lot less. I know that during the same time that I had no attraction to any other girls. It's real hard to say yes or no, but I think the possibility would have been very low."

His relationship with his oldest daughter following the abuse

"My daughters never testified in court because I agreed to a plea bargain. I have statements from them. But nothing was ever brought up in court. My older daughter did make a statement in court that she wanted something to happen, but she didn't want a lot because like I said, at this point we had reached a point where we had communicated and talked about what had happened. I started making a concerted effort to not put myself in a position where she would be in any way fearful. I would stop hugging her. I stopped, you know, being very close to her. The only time I really showed affection for her was in public. I think she showed that she still had some concern for me.

"We had a discussion when she was, oh, the last half of her senior year just before she was getting ready to go to college. She had already found out she had a scholarship to go to college. We had a discussion. We talked about an hour about what had happened. What my feelings were, and hers, and things that had gone on. She pretty much made it clear that she had never wanted it; she didn't want it to go on, she wanted us to have a relationship that was normal, you know, father and a daughter, not with anything else involved, and that we needed to make a change. I agreed. She told me that I needed to make a change in myself. It was about two and a half years after our discussion that I started molesting my younger daughter."

Offender #4

Introduction

Offender #4 is a white 34-year-old female who has served one and a half years of a four year sentence at the time of this interview. She is married and has three children, two girls 14 and 15 years old and a boy who is 12. She was charged with sexual assault on a child. She began to fondle and perform oral sex on her son when he was eight years old and continued to abuse him for four years.

The Interview

Her abusive childhood

"I was abused by my stepfather and three other men. One was a cousin of mine and the other two were my dad's friends. It started when I was five years old and continued until I was 15. My parents told me that the reason why I was doing this at age five was to help their financial situation. This was my way of helping the family to get money for food and clothing. People were paying my parents to sexually molest me."

Her husband's abuse of her daughters

"I never sexually abused my daughters but my husband did sexually abuse them. I was aware of it but I didn't stop the situation. The girls were eight and nine at the time. One day my husband just told me he was sexually abusing the girls. He had oral sex with them, the whole thing. He had intercourse with the girls. He said he had been doing it for a couple months. I was angry with him when he was telling me what he was doing, but I just looked at him and I walked away. I didn't say anything to him. Like I said before, when I was being sexually abused as a child, my parents would tell me what I was doing was right. So I figure what I was doing in my household was okay. When I was a kid my mom knew I was being abused and so did my dad, my real dad. They would tell me, there is nothing wrong with this.

"So when I found out my husband was abusing the girls I perceived it as whatever is happening in the home was okay. I didn't think of it as being wrong. It was right there in the home and nobody else was getting hurt. I wasn't thinking that they were getting hurt. They never talked to me about it. So I just closed off to it, because I felt there was nothing wrong with it because I went through the same thing when I was their age."

Her relationship with her eight-year-old son

"Before the abuse I had a pretty good relationship with my son. We got along great. We did a lot of outdoor sports together. I would take him to his Boy Scout meetings and stuff. Normally we got along great. The only time that he got upset with me and didn't want to be around me is when I would abuse him, which I couldn't blame him. He would talk to me, but he didn't want to be around me."

The sexual abuse of her eight-year-old son

"How that started is one day I was in my home; I was talking to my mom on the phone and I got angry because she asked me to give somebody another chance and I wouldn't do that. She got mad at me, and I got mad at her, and I hung up. I took my anger out on my son. I would fondle him and perform oral sex on him. That would be the only time I would sexually abuse him, when I was angry. I took that out on him. When I did things to my son I wasn't angry at him. I was angry at what my mother wanted me to do.

"I never physically hit him when I was angry. I think I sexually assaulted him because that is what was done to me at his age. I was abused in that same way and I put him through the same thing. Sometimes I would abuse him twice in a month. It depended on what I was doing or how angry I was with my mom or the person I was talking to on the phone that set me off.

"The abuse would go for about 15 minutes. Sometimes that's all I did was just fondle him. Then there were other times I just performed oral sex on him. I would do this in his room. He would tell me 'no,' and he would start crying and that, and I just didn't pay any attention to it at the time. I just continued until I thought it was enough, then I quit and walked away from it.

"After a while his behavior changed. He never said no anymore. He just laid there and never said anything to me anymore. But he never pulled away from me. He quit pulling away from me. He'd come up and talk to me afterwards. And he asked, well can I go out and ride on my bike or whatever? I'd say, sure, you know.

"Prior to doing the sexual abuse on him I was looking forward to what I was going to be doing with him. And while I was abusing him I was enjoying what I was doing. Afterwards I was angry at myself. I was just miserable, I hated myself for it. I knew what I was doing hurt him. I did it anyway. I got so angry I would hurt him, but I didn't want to hurt him anymore. I wanted to put a stop to it and I didn't want to do any more sexual abuse to him. I didn't want to hurt him anymore.

"I don't think I rationalized it. I wasn't thinking very clearly. It was poor judgment on my behalf taking my anger out on him when he had nothing to do with it. I never saw myself enjoying what I was doing. I knew it was wrong but I did it anyway. I wanted…I guess what I was looking at, I wanted somebody else to know what I was going through, the pain I was going through. And that person was my son."

What precipitated the sexual abuse

"The only reason I can think of that I abused my son and not my daughters is because I was angry at men because of the abuse I went through. When I got angry, he was there. And the girls, I never thought about doing anything to them.

"Before I started abusing Cody I used to get angry but I just did a lot of cleaning. I bottled all my anger up inside me to where I shut down, to where I wouldn't talk to anybody. I'd just give in to what everybody wanted me to do at that time. Then when I started to abuse Cody I felt like

I had just had enough. I was so angry and I took my anger out on him. I hurt him. He would tell me 'no,' and I wouldn't listen. He was crying and he was upset. But I just kept doing it anyway because I was already angry and I didn't care.

"There were a variety of different things that would trigger my anger. I didn't start abusing my son until he was eight years old. I think the reason I didn't abuse him the first eight years was because in those 8 years my mom wasn't here in the state. She had moved to Arizona and she wasn't around me very much. When she came back from Arizona to live here, that's when it all started and it went on until he was 12 years old.

"It was when I talked to my mother that a lot of things got stirred up. I didn't talk to her very much though. It was when I talked to her that's when I got so mad and angry, and I would take it out on my son."

Her interview with the police

"A detective came to our house to talk to us. I denied that I was doing anything wrong. I denied that anything was going on in the home. They came out and they talked to the kids first that evening. The kids said nothing; they said nothing happened. About three months down the road the detective called us to a shelter for children to come and be able to have a place, a safe place to talk. He talked to me and he talked to my daughter, Crystal. I denied it then too, that anything took place. And Crystal even did the same thing. And they didn't get anything from us until they talked to my husband. My husband confessed what he did. He confessed because he didn't want to hurt them anymore. He was tired of hurting the girls. He also told them I was molesting Cody.

“They arrested my husband that day. I didn’t get arrested until three months later. It was in March, because my son told him what took place. The kids were in a foster home at that time. That’s why I’m in here now. Because I’m facing up to what I did was wrong.

“When the police first talked to me I didn’t admit anything because I didn’t want to admit what I was doing was wrong. I wanted to be left alone and figure I can handle it myself, fix the situation myself. They tried to say, well, this is what your husband was saying. And I’m like I don’t believe my husband would be doing this to me. So I didn’t fall for what they were saying. I wasn’t going to go in there and say anything. I have a hard time with the police department anyway, because one of the men who molested me was a cop. So I have a hard time believing what cops were telling me on the other end. I would have been more comfortable with a female cop because of what I’ve gone through. I think it would be better sometimes to have another female in there asking the questions. I would probably open up more with a female, because that female may have been abused themselves.”

Offender #5

Introduction

Offender #5 is a 51-year-old white male serving time for sexually molesting prepubescent boys ages 11 to 13 years old. He was arrested in 1995 and was in his fifth year of his sentence at the time of this interview. He was married one time from 1975 to 1982. He served 20 years in the military. After leaving the military he started to sexually molest pre-pubescent boys. He would carry on this abusive relationship with each of his victims for about two years.

The Interview

The grooming behaviors, setup and progression of the sexual abuse

"I think it's probably important to tell you first that when I was going through high school, junior high school, I would always have young male friends around me. What I'm seeing now is I've got an issue with low self-worth. And these young boys would be around 11, 12, 13 years old, would look up to me and they'd make me feel good. They liked hanging out with the big guy, or the guy that drives.

"My first victim was a neighbor child. I perceived him to be having problems with the family. He was looking for affection. I used that to put like a wedge between his father and him. I groomed him, paid a lot of attention to him, and eventually started talking to him about sexual things. He was 12, just 12 years old at the time. I took advantage of his interest, and him growing in his maturity. I eventually started molesting him. I was 15 years old at the time.

"I learned real early that they would make me feel good, and I'd engage them in sexual talk, and what I thought at the time was mutual masturbation, things like that. Looking back at it, though, I can see how that was a pattern that I was developing even back then. My first victim as an adult was when I was around 30 years old.

"It was a young boy that was delivering newspapers. When I saw him my first thought was that he was, you know, attractive. I would start talking to him. It was a slow process. You know, he'd come by and he'd collect once a month; I'd pay him. I would ask him if he would like to help around the house, make a little extra money, okay, and those things. So once he was there I'd always stop and pay attention to him, talk to him, and joke around with him, things like that, trying to be the good, the nice guy, gain his trust. Then I got closer to the mother; I found out that he was from a single parent. I befriended the mother. Eventually we started doing some other things, maybe go to a movie, something like that. And that process went on for I'd say three to four months. Then he would come over more regularly. I would start talking to him about sexual things and eventually I started molesting him.

"I would initiate the discussions about sex. I might say something… like if I see him touching himself or grabbing at himself, I might say something like, 'well don't worry, it will grow,' try to break the ice a little bit or something to that effect. Or I might say, 'you must be growing some hair now, are you itching?' things like that. Then, try to, try to manipulate a confidence, if you would, to get him to possibly open up and even want to talk more.

"There would be a period of where I would start wrestling with him, tickling him. It would be a process of breaking boundaries. If he wouldn't want me to, say, tickle him, I'd stop. Or if he did, I might tickle him a little closer down to his genitals. I was always aware that if he didn't want to, I would stop. And then the next time maybe break the boundary a little bit more. This went on for about was about six months before I started molesting him.

"I had a vibrator. I laid that out one day, and he had seen that. Apparently he already knew what it was, what it was for. I asked him if he'd be interested in using it. At that point he wanted to but he didn't want me to be there. So that was another progression of breaking boundaries.

"The next time that happened I can't remember exactly how it was but I had said to him, 'well, you know, you've already used it, I might as well help you' or something like that. But that was another way just to gradually break him down. I held the vibrator, showed him where to put it, and then later I physically touched him. Afterwards, when I talked to him I would ask him, 'well was that good? Did you enjoy it?' He said he did. I'm sure there was some confusion. I'm sure that it did feel good, but yet there was probably a tremendous amount of confusion as to why is this guy doing this? It wasn't my intention to make him think it was his fault. But he would say things like he enjoyed that, or you know, I would make sure to remind him that he said, 'well it felt good.' Okay? But as far as making him believe that the whole thing was his fault, I never rationally thought about it that way with him. I think the manipulation and the calculated way that I was doing it all plays into it, though.

"After the first time that I assaulted him, I would usually try to do something with him over the next hour, hour and a half, that wasn't anything related to sexual things. It might be play a video game, something that I had remembered that he might especially like. It might be go get, go down to get a hamburger or something. That reassured me that he would be okay, he wouldn't tell, basically. If he appeared upset, then we could talk a little bit before. I believe for me that was my way to make him think that this wasn't the only thing I wanted him around for. Then the next time it was easier to break the boundary. That led up to other sexual activity that included oral sex and, uh, digital penetration.

"I took a couple of Polaroid pictures of him while he was engaging in sexual behavior. I used these pictures as visual stimulus when he wasn't around. I would masturbate to them. I molested this boy over about a two-year period. I didn't sodomize the paperboy but I did sodomize some of my victims. I would start maybe with digital penetration. Then later I would penetrate them anally. There were a couple of the boys that didn't want to do that so I didn't pursue it. Some of the other boys, they seemed to find it a little exciting for them.

At first I would start with thinking, gee, if I could just see this kid naked. Okay? Well, once I did that, I would think if I could just touch them, then I would think, if I could just masturbate them. It was never enough. Finally I began to digital penetrate and then sodomize them.

Why he began molesting children in his thirties

"I think a big part of that was being in the military. I did really well in a structured environment. A lot of this happened as I got ready to get out and once I was out of the service. One of the things I'm finding out with myself here is that I've always lived in a stressful environment. My father was an alcoholic who would beat my mom. Later I found out that he was forcing himself on her. I left that environment, went into the Air Force. The Air Force created a lot of stress for me just by the nature of the job. I was married and then went through a divorce while in the military. And once I got out it was like I didn't have all this stress, so I was creating stress, by having several jobs. I never really learned how to relax.

"I was about two or three years from getting out of the military when I met the paperboy. I think for me, even through this whole period where I didn't assault anybody, I would have a lot of fantasy life in my mind. I would run through scenarios in my mind of how I would, you know, like to do this, or like to do that with a young boy. I would fantasize about performing oral sex on a boy or me receiving oral sex from the boy."

How he manipulated his victims to insure non-disclosure

"I never threatened him. I never said anything to him like, 'If you tell, I'm going to be in trouble.' I believe that the boys that I targeted were starving so much for affection, for someone to pay attention to them.

"As the paperboy started getting interested in girls he would just say, 'I don't want to do this anymore.' And because he was growing out of what I preferred as a victim I thought that was fine. He would keep coming back over with his girlfriends. In my distorted way of thinking I was taking that like I didn't hurt this kid, he's doing good in school, he's got girlfriends, he's good in sports. So it was easy for me to not think of myself as a child molester.

"I thought that he still cared for me, still liked me, and that he was probably thinking of it as just something that happened, no big deal. Again, I never threatened them. If after the assaults started there might be times where they might call and say, 'Hey, I need to go down here to pick this up or something, Mom's busy; do you think you can do it?' And even if I had something that I needed to do or other plans, I would stop basically what I was doing to be there. Again, it wasn't really specifically for them, but I knew that I would be doing something that I'd get that payoff of feeling important again. It was another way to groom knowing that any time he would need something I would be there. I think for me it boiled down to that the boys that I selected in the initial grooming were all boys that were, they had such a void in their life, again, and that they were willing to put up with the negative, the sexual abuse, for the other affection.

"Out of all the boys I molested there was only one that after he had gone away and come back from college to talk to me about it. We talked about it a little bit but I was more in like a clean up mode at that time. I could sense something from the conversation that he wasn't real happy. I wasn't so much worried that he was going to tell, but I had to cleanup the fact that I had abused him by trying to do some more grooming. He was upset, and didn't say much. And so I looked at him; I said, 'I'm sorry.' And he said, 'Well, I needed to hear that.' I said, 'It wasn't your fault.' And then he left; I didn't see him again. I can only imagine some of the things that went through his mind."

His adult sexual relationships

"There was one occasion I did have a sexual encounter with an adult male that was 18. His appearance was of that of a much younger male. This happened shortly after my divorce. There was this guy who worked for me. He was 18 years old. Everybody used to kid him, do you have a note from your mom to be in the service, that type of thing. He looked real young. After my divorce I asked him to move in with me. And this is something that I'm seeing now, the unequal power base that I had over the children. I used the same thing with him. I was his boss; he lived in my house. So there wasn't an equal power relationship at all there.

"When I got married I was definitely in love. My wife and I did have a satisfying sexual relationship as I look back. I met my wife while I was in the service. I had a break in the service and went to college, that's where I met her. She was five years younger than I was and I can look back and see again there was an unequal power base. I was 23 and she was 18. That put me in the position of being the one that was in charge. The military took her away from her family so I isolated her from there. So she had to be totally dependent on me. I was not, by any stretch of the imagination, a good husband. I would make her feel guilty with things that I say, and a lot of it around sex. You know, 'We don't have sex anymore,' or, 'You don't give me head anymore'; things like that trying to make her feel bad. Eventually I tried to make her feel guilty enough to where we would have sex. It wasn't any more satisfying for me that way because I could see that she didn't want to do it. I basically after a few times like that, I discontinued doing that. We got divorced when I was about 30. During my eight years of marriage I did have sex with other women. But I would still have fantasies of, and masturbate, and reinforce that, to adolescent boys. I might have seen a boy on TV that I would fantasize about. I look back at some of my sexual history that I put out. I've had prostitutes, when I was over in Korea, over in Germany. For me, it's, you know, sex meets all needs."

The various types of sexual abuse he engaged in

"It was shortly after that is when I found another family, very similar. The family was similar in the way that the child wasn't getting paid a lot of attention. He lived with his mom and dad and I started the same process again, started befriending them, and started doing things with them. Eventually I started molesting him. His dad was a work associate. I basically repeated the whole process. And that would be a pattern that I'd use with three other boys following this one. I have sexually assaulted a total of seven boys. I molested each of them for approximately a year to 18 months. The assaults would usually end with them growing out of that age I was attracted to and them being more interested in girls. At least I think I was losing interest. But there would be times where they might come back over and it might be two or three months since the last assault. I would assault them again. So I don't know if it was so much me losing interest. I think in my manipulative thinking that what I was doing was trying to make it feel that they were, had some kind of control over this. If they felt that they had some kind of control, then they could stop anytime.

"This does not take into account the number of boys I had wrestled with and then touched them for my own gratification. I assumed that they didn't even realize what I was doing. If I included that type of abuse there's about another 10 boys. And some of these were during that period when I got divorced, up to when I actually assaulted. One that I can recall was at a friend's place where there was a swimming pool there. One of the kids was in the swimming pool; it was a boy, roughly 12 or 13. I didn't know him, but I started picking him up, throwing him. He wanted to horseplay in the pool so I was able to pick him up, and push him by the butt. Or when he would try to put, dunk me under the water I might go to touch his privates."

His rationalizations for his abusive behavior

"I first would justify it by thinking I wasn't hurting them, okay, that they liked it. My thoughts would be around the fact that if they would come back, that I didn't hurt them, that they liked it. I knew that it was wrong, but because I didn't believe I was hurting, I discounted the fact that I was breaking the law. I discounted the fact that I was manipulating and victimizing these young boys just because that's what I wanted.

Because I wanted to molest them I would find reasons to justify it. As long as they kept coming back I thought it was not hurting them. If they would say to me that they didn't want to do anything, I would stop. But I knew that maybe later, even in the same day, that I would attempt to assault them again.

"Again, I rationalized it by believing I wasn't hurting them, believing that I did care about them, that I did like them. I could never accept what I was doing. I would never look at what I was doing as, all the manipulation I used, the things that I've explained here that I've been able to learn about myself through treatment, I just never, never looked at that. It was definitely self-serving, but I was able to rationalize it because they did keep coming back over. And after the second boy, and the third boy, and the patterns were all the same and they all continued to come around, it was pretty easy for me. That was all the justification I needed."

What precipitated his abusive behavior

"I do see that there seems to be a pattern. I really have an issue with thinking that I'm a worthless person, that I can't do anything right. And when these kids would make me feel like somebody important the payoff that I was getting in addition to sexual payoff was that they would say things to me like, 'Man I wish you were my dad' or, 'I wish I could live with you,' things like that. So it made me feel like I was somebody to these kids. And for me with distortions of sex meeting all needs, I figured, and also distorted thinking that goes like, love equals sex, affection equals sex, and all these are distorted ways of thinking that I would use. So that's where I felt that entitlement to molest. I don't know if that made sense or not."

How he felt about his abusive behavior

"Immediately after the abuse there was a satisfaction. Then I would feel guilt, and I would go through a period of, 'oh, I'm not going to do that anymore.' But this feeling of guilt didn't last very long. Sometimes it would last just a few hours. I think that's another reason why I would be very calculated with when I would make the choice to molest them so that I knew there would be some time afterwards that I could continue to groom them to make sure that when they left that that wasn't the last thing they left with. I could probably say that this was for their benefit, but it was all self-serving. Everything I did was for me."

His abusive childhood

"When I was 11, I was with a 15-year-old male cousin. I never thought of it as anything until after doing some treatment, and looking back there. I was pretty naïve at that age. My male cousin wanted me to masturbate him and he masturbated me. To the best of my recollection there was a pleasure there but there was confusion. It felt good, but yet I didn't understand it. This was the only time something like this happened. This happened at a time where in my family I wasn't getting a lot of affection either.

"I have a sister that's four years older and then a brother that's 13 years younger. I was an average student. I didn't put a lot of effort in it; I could have done a lot better. I played some sports, and was involved in music. My parents had so many issues of their own that I was just there. They fought a lot. I think my father abused alcohol and he would physically abuse my mother and my sister, not so much with me."

His preferred victim

"It's not so much the age of the boys I look for but their features, boys that are just getting into puberty, not quite developed yet. With different boys I think, you know, it happens at different times. So, it's more of the features versus the actual age. But, prepubescent to, you know, the early years, 12 to 13 years old.

"While I have been here they have us go through what they call a sexual cycle here. When I went through that it was a pretty intense group for me. I spent six months going through my life from beginning to end. And in that group the other members, there are five or so other sex offenders there, and they challenge a lot of my distorted thinking. At that point it had been 'my story, so I'm sticking to it,' type of thing; and they challenged me. The awareness that I got was when I sat there…there's a part where we describe our preferred victim, not so much our victim pool, but the preferred victim. When I went down and I looked at that, and I read that in the group, and I thought after that, I go…my God, that was me when I was 11 years old which was kind of freaky.

"The boy that I explained as my preferred victim was who I was at 11 years old. And so I've explored that, and that's where I've been able to build off that cycle, seeing the vulnerabilities that I chose. There's always, there's a little, for lack of better words, a little independence, a little smart-alecky, a little cockiness. There's willingness to be on the edge a little bit. And even when I was a youngster I was keeping secrets, you know. I was already learning a secretive lifestyle. The boys I molested had a lot of the same things going on in their family that went on with mine when I was their age."

His opinion regarding legal age of consent

> Note: The age of consent differs from state to state. At the time of this interview the age of consent in Hawaii was 14 years old[8], the lowest in the United States. When offender #5 was advised of this he began to visibly breathe heavy and responded as follows:

"Well, you know, inside I was feeling a little nervousness there. Because I've learned now, and I touched on it a little bit before, about the unequal power base. And um, it's...the relationship has to be equal. And I just don't see that anybody that is older than an individual like that could be working from an equal power base. That shouldn't be. Because I think what that does is allows perpetration. This is where I'm at now. Seven or eight years ago I would have found that arousing and exciting."

His interview with the police

"With the boy that I was arrested for the discovery came when the father came over to the house. This gets back to the neighbor boy. We had just gotten out of the hot tub. The father was upset, and he says, 'gee, what's going on here?' And the son said, 'Nothing's going on.' The boy was helping me deliver newspapers. That was one of the ways that I had groomed this boy. So, after the newspaper in the morning we got in the tub in our suits. His father was coming over to get him, because he was a

[8] That law has since been repealed and the legal age of consent in Hawaii is 16 years old at the time of this writing.

little longer. I think he had suspicions; I believe the discovery came about 10 days later. I had been assaulting this boy for about three months.

"When the police came, the investigation had already been done. And they went ahead and arrested me for sexual assault. I think what happened was, and I can only speculate here, but I believe this boy was already seeing a psychiatrist for something. I don't know if there were some problems going on. The discovery, we found out, was not through the normal channels like through Social Services. It came in from another avenue. So we believe the discovery came that way.

"Initially when they arrested me I said I didn't do this. I answered the basic questions. But when there were other questions that I didn't feel comfortable with, I decided I would, you know, should have an attorney. I was very nervous. I knew that I was in serious trouble.

"After I was released on bond, and was talking with my lawyer, we were trying to work a plea agreement out. I didn't want to go to trial. I figured at that point that I really needed to deal with this, because if I didn't, I was just going to continue to do it. I had to get out of the denial. That actually took quite a bit longer after. Saying I did it was one thing, but then what I was really doing was trying to make the consequence have the least affect on me. Again, it had nothing to do with doing the right thing. It was, again, damage control type of thinking. So I admitted it to my attorney and he worked out a plea bargain with the prosecutor.

His advice for police interrogations

Thinking about how I was at the time I was arrested, I would think it would be really hard if a person is in denial to get them to admit anything. I think a person is so basically hell-bent on believing themselves that they weren't hurting anyone or that they didn't do things at all. I know I worked off a premise of a real lack of trust in any authority figure. I would not have looked at the interrogator as a friend at all. You know, I would have looked at the interrogator, investigator, whatever as basically doing whatever he needed to do to get an admission.

"Like I said, I work off of a lack of trust. It wouldn't have mattered if it was just you or two people in there, in that situation I'm not in control. So, for me, I'm going to shut up. If there's a way to get that, get the offender to understand that if he does admit it, that he can take some control of the situation, it might make a difference. I think that that might be a key. I believe for me, even when I was being interviewed by the police, I knew that I was going to take ownership eventually down the road, but I was going to do it on my terms. And I think that's where it was, even though that's a false sense of security, when I was with the attorney and talking to him, there was a sense that I'm in control of a bad situation.

"My biggest fear of admitting the abuse I would have to say was going to prison. That for me ties into fear of the unknown. After being in prison, I don't think that's a deterrent anymore. The fact of going to prison wouldn't be enough to keep me from re-offending.

"I'm glad I understand that, because I don't want to spend my life like this. So, by understanding that prison wouldn't be the deterrent, I have to find out what's really going on inside. I don't want to hurt anybody anymore. I know that may sound canned, but my family's been affected. The people that I've assaulted have been affected. He may be walking around today and smell somebody that wore the same cologne I wore and all that's going to come back to him."

Offender #6

Introduction

Offender #6 is a 26-year-old white female who sexually assaulted a 14-year-old boy when she was 24 years old. She is divorced with three children — a four-month-old boy, one-year-old girl, and a four-year-old boy. She had been married for seven years. She was originally arrested on five felony counts of sexual assault on a minor in a position of trust. A plea-bargain was arranged and she pleaded guilty to one count of sexual assault on a 14-year-old male. Since she has been in prison she has acknowledged that she had two other victims, a 14-year-old female and a 17-year-old male. She said the only sexual contact she had with the 14-year-old female was kissing at a few parties and she "dated" a 17-year-old male for about eight months prior to meeting the victim of record. She is scheduled to be released in two weeks after serving two and a half years at the facility.

The Interview

Her marriage

"I got married when I just turned 18. I was six months pregnant at the time. For the most part we shared in responsibilities. I took care of the money, finances, and things like that. Then my husband started cheating on me quite a few times. There was never any drug use. Once in a while we would go to a bar, to a club, and have some drinks or whatever. Drinking at home, there usually really wasn't any drinking at home, because we just didn't feel the need, I guess. It was a physically abusive relationship, verbally abusive relationship, mentally abusive. He verbally abused my oldest but other than that it was just me.

"A couple times the police had to come out to our house. There was a restraining order issued for a certain period of time, and then we'd both go to court and I'd say that I wanted the restraining order dropped. I needed him home because of the kids. So it was just that rotating cycle that just kept on going.

"One time I was in the hospital with a really bad infection that I could have died from. It had poisoned my bloodstream. I had just had my last son and I had gotten a bladder infection that turned into a kidney infection. And while I was in the hospital he's out cheating on me with some girl at the house. My friend told me about it. So when I got out of the hospital I kicked him out, told him get out, put all of his stuff out on the porch, and changed the locks on the doors. He had a girlfriend so he had somewhere to go. I threatened him with calling the cops and getting a restraining order on him. We've been separated ever since."

The sexual abuse of a 14-year-old boy

"In September I had kicked my husband out of the house and filed for divorce and the whole bit. I have three minor children, and at the time they were just like four months old, one year old, and like four years old. I was working, trying to pay bills, and stuff like that. I needed somebody to be there at the house to baby-sit the kids while I was gone at work. So, one of my friends' little sisters, who was 14 years old, her mom said that it was okay that if she came and stayed with me. Because her mom was having problems with her in school, skipping school, and just a lot of family problems. Her mom was just like, yeah, if you think you can handle her, take her. So she moved in with me.

"She was watching the kids when I would go to work. She was doing good. She was going to school, you know, and there were certain rules that she had to follow. Well, after probably about a month of this I would start to come home from work and she would have friends over at the house that were also in her age group, 14, 15, 16 years old. So there was a lot of partying with her having friends over. That's actually how I met Doug, which was my 14-year-old victim. I allowed them to have parties at the house. It kind of fit into what I wanted. I justified that also by saying that I would rather them be there at the house partying than out driving drunk, and you know, the whole bit. It just went from there. It escalated from there probably about a month, month-and-a-half after Doug and everybody else were coming over all the time. He and I began this relationship-type thing. After a while he was staying at my house because his mother was in the county jail and he didn't want to stay with his grandmother. So he and his brother stayed at my house. So they were staying at my house, and he and I were in a relationship with each other.

"It started out just flirting, playing around, wrestling around. Just, actually like kids do. I was a kid. I was acting like a kid, you know. It was flirting, it was the back-and-forth. He would be there and be taking care of the kids, and you know, everybody pitched in to help out with the kids and stuff. So that was like a quality that I was, you know, attracted to. That the kids liked him and he liked the kids. Well, of course, because he was a kid himself, you know, so of course the kids are going to like him. But, it just went from there. I liked him and I wanted to be in a relationship with him.

"His cousin Josh told me, actually, that Doug liked me. I thought he was cute; he looked older, probably 17, not of age, but probably 17-18. I knew he was only 14 but after Josh had told me that Doug had liked me, then I started looking at him differently. It was like an open door to me.

"One night there was a party at my house, and we were all playing cards. And we were sitting next to each other. He had put his hand on my leg, and we just, you know, were looking at each other and kind of laughing. And everything was just like everybody was there, and everybody was partying, and everybody was, you know, with their boyfriend or their girlfriend or whatever, and we all started playing a truth and dare game. One of his friends had dared him and I to kiss. And so we kissed. And then later that night after everybody was like either passing out, or going home, or whatever, then him and I ended up going to my room and we ended up having sexual intercourse then. We had sex about three or four times a week for about six months.

"Physically, I would have to say he made the first move. But, I was the adult, so I should have had those boundaries to stop it. He would make the first moves. But, it was both of us, you know. This went on for about six months. His age didn't enter my mind. It was like, to me I felt like we were both consenting it so that it was an okay thing. You know, the age, it wasn't even a factor in my mind.

"Everybody knew. We didn't keep it hid or anything. And to me, while I was in the relationship I enjoyed it. He got along with the kids, and the kids got along with him, and he treated me good, and he was always telling me I was pretty, and how good I am. It was like that dream relationship, I thought at the time. And the age factor never came into my mind. It never, you know, it never occurred to me that, you know, he's a child, and he goes to school, and the whole bit. I didn't think about that.

"It was like it fulfilled my weaknesses and my feeling of loss of power and control, because he would like brag about the relationship. You know, I mean, here he is 14 and he's with a 24-year-old. He's got a girlfriend who will get us our beer or whatever. I could supply them a house to party at. I was the cool person, and I had a vehicle, and I could go pick up his friends for him, so I think for him he viewed it as something, you know, like wow, my girlfriend can do all this, and this and this.

"I didn't hide the relationship. It was like everybody knew that him and I were together. Everybody, all of my friends, all of his friends, people in the community. We'd go places together holding hands or whatever."

How she manipulated her victim and rationalized her abusive behavior

"I think the reason I acted on my attraction to Doug was probably because he was acting on it with me. It was, it was something that I didn't feel like I was going to be rejected on. So, it was that open door. I think I might have seen Doug as a safe relationship. I don't think that I was afraid of him physically. I don't think I was afraid of him leaving me or cheating on me.

"Our relationship filled my feelings of loneliness, feeling unwanted, abandoned. I think it filled more of an emotional need for me than a sexual need. I'm sure there was an adult male who could have done the same thing but that's not what I was looking for. I feel that I was looking for someone that was easily manipulated. That would be easy for me to manipulate to gain whatever I needed to gain. Because what adult male is going to allow a bunch of partying, and you know, friends over all the time, and the drugs, and alcohol, and all of that? They're not. You know, the kids, 14-15-16-17, that's what they're looking for. When I was in the relationship with Jim prior to Doug, Jim introduced me to methamphetamines. Probably about a week after I tried meth for my first time I started buying large quantities of it and distributing it myself. A couple years down the road, I furthered on to manufacturing. When Doug was there with his friends, methamphetamines were there quite a bit; marijuana also. Doug's brother, Barry, would go with me whenever I would be going to sell large amounts and was like my bodyguard or whatever.

"I rationalized my relationship with Doug by telling myself he made me feel good about myself, that there was always people over at the house, you know, his friends. I felt popular, I felt well-liked, and the loneliness wasn't there. I felt that he was a friend that I could talk to about problems that I was going through. I rationalized it by just all of that, you know, making it like this was a relationship I wanted to be in forever. I didn't think that what I was doing was wrong, you know, especially with his mom knowing and stuff; I didn't think it was wrong. No one ever approached me to say this was wrong. There were people who didn't care for the group of people that I was hanging out with, like my grandmother.

She didn't like Doug at all. She thought he was a smart ass, excuse me, smart alec, and just didn't care for him or his group of friends, you know. So she would talk to me about that but she would never talk any further.

"I think even if I knew it was against the law it wouldn't have changed anything. Because, like I said, that age group was just the group that I was looking for that I knew that I could manipulate easily. I knew that I could use that power. I've got the vehicle, I've got the house, I can buy your alcohol, I can supply the drugs, I can, you know, all of that. So that was just the age group that I was looking for."

Her interview with the police

"When his mom got out of the county jail she brought cops over to the house. It all came out and I got arrested on charges of the sexual assault. The night I was arrested I had been out with a friend to another town to do a drop delivery of some meth. I had left Doug and his cousin Zach at my house to watch the kids. It was like 11:00 at night and the kids were in bed. So I left them there to watch the kids. Well, it turned out that Zach was a runaway. And Doug, his mom was looking for him also. So, Doug's mom told the cops to look for him over at my house, that he'd probably be there. So the cops came over to my house. Well, when the cops got there Doug and Zach were drinking 40-ounce beers that I had in the refrigerator. The police took them into custody. Of course, they were drinking underage, and one was on the run, you know. So they took them into custody and called Social Services. Social Services came and got my kids. Two of the kids were there, my other child, my oldest, was at his grandma's. They went later on in the night and got him from there.

"So I came home to an empty house. I called the police station because they had left a card for me to call them. I went down there, and they talked to me about what they had found when they got to the house, and told me that the kids were in custody with Social Services. They said that I would have to call the next day to try and get them out. That's actually how everything started. Social Services had the kids, they were getting ready to give them back to me, it was probably almost two weeks later, and that's when they came and arrested me on these charges of sexual assault.

"Doug's mom told the police about me and him. Because she had came over one morning and Barry, Doug's brother, had let his mom into the house. And Doug and I were in bed together.

"I, one thing that I would like to say about the police is that, I'm not going to say that they were responsible for any of my offenses, because they weren't; I was totally responsible for that. But one thing that I would suggest is that when you're going to a house and you're breaking up parties that consist of one adult, which in my situation was me, and the entire house is filled with 13-14-15-16-17-year-olds and you're continuously going to that house and breaking up parties, intervene, try to intervene then. I'm not...they're not responsible for my offenses, but what I'm saying is that I think that if they would have intervened sooner, maybe it could have stopped me. That's all I'm saying. Ask yourself a question, why is this 24-year-old cruising Main Street with all these kids in her vehicle? Why is she going to keggers out in the mountains with 13 and 14-year-olds? Why are the only people at her house 13 and 14 and 15-year- olds? Ask yourself that and intervene."

Offender #7

Introduction

Offender #7 is a 40-year-old white female. She is married and has three children of her own and three stepchildren. She participated in the sexual abuse of her 16-year-old stepdaughter who was the biological daughter of her husband. She and her husband were also involved in the manufacture and distribution of methamphetamines.

The Interview

Her description of her marriage and family

"I was living with a gentleman; we were common-law I guess. We owned a big ol' 80-acre ranch. We owned a big home, a five-bedroom, three-bath tri-level home. The kids were very well taken care of. We made $2,000 a month just off of one cattle lease. We were both raised in the country, and knew the ranching lifestyle. My common-law husband was a master plumber, and he and I both worked. Even though we were doing a lot of drugs, we were very productive drug users.

"He had a 14-year-old daughter. We were heavy into drugs. There was a lot of drug use. As a result of the drug use there was a lot of abuse in the home against me and his 14-year-old daughter. As a result of me being tired and fighting with him I sat in a room and allowed him to rape his daughter and did nothing to stop it. I was very angry. I was using drugs, but I don't use drugs as an excuse for my behavior. I know that I made a wrong decision, and I know that I chose to make that decision. I know better than to have done what I did. There's things that I'm learning about myself and my cycle to not repeat that type of decision-making or to ever allow myself to be in that situation again.

"I had been living with my common-law husband for about five years. He started to sexually abuse his 14-year-old daughter about three and a half years after we started living together. There were seven children in the home. I have three biological children of my own, he had four children; three of them were girls and one was a boy. I had two boys and a girl. My daughter was a couple of years younger than his daughter he abused. None of the other children were abused. They would always be in their rooms sleeping when Jodi was being abused.

"I think he had been abusing her before I found out. I just don't think that I recognized it. I believed that it was always there. After we were arrested I found out that he had been molesting her prior to my ever knowing him, when he lived with the child's real mother, the biological mother. He got custody of his children because the mother ran off and it had never gone to court, or nothing like. I found out about the earlier abuse through the court proceedings. We had separate trials and I found out from my lawyer.

"We were originally got in trouble for some other stuff. I had caused us to get arrested through some drug stuff. I was tired, I was scared, and I didn't know what to do. I intentionally had gotten us in trouble. We were in jail because we were bouncing checks back and forth from account to account in our own personal account. Since we were in jail the kids were staying with family. Jodi told her aunt what her father had done to her and she reported it to Social Services.

"He was still incarcerated at the time and I was out, um, on ISP probation. My parole officer called me in, and I went and talked to her. She told me what had been reported. And I told her, that yeah, that the incident did occur, but at the time I was in denial and I was like, well I didn't do anything to her, I didn't touch her, I didn't sexually assault her. An investigator talked to me, and they let me go. The investigator just told me, you know, you need to stay around until this is investigated further.

"At the time I would not admit that I was the one that went and got her and brought her into the room. I just said that, yeah, it happened, and he did it, and I didn't have nothing to do with it. Because I was in denial I didn't see myself as being a sex offender. Just because I didn't engage in sexual contact with her, I was in denial about myself. I kept pleading my innocence and blaming it all on him. After I had first been arrested, Jodi was saying that her mother had done things to her also. It came out later that she was referring to her biological mom and not me so those things were dismissed out of court."

Her abusive relationship with her husband

"He would physically abuse me. The children had probably been awakened many nights by the fighting and the arguing going on, and me being beat up by him. I've had all my front teeth knocked out by this man. I was very abused by him. The first three years there weren't any problems. I mean, there was like maybe some verbal things or whatever normal things that a couple would go through, fighting about bills or something like that. But then the drug and alcohol usage came into play in the relationship. The relationship became very sexual and I was being raped by this gentleman. We started to watch pornographic movies after the drugs became introduced into our relationship. One night when we were getting high on methamphetamine, he told me that he felt as if Jodi was trying to approach him, or making sexual advances towards him. And we got into a big ol' fight about it. As a result of it I ended up being raped by him that night. This then started out to be the cycle. He became obsessed with it. He was constantly talking to me about it. And in my own mind I was trying to justify what he was saying and didn't want to admit to myself that, hey you know, this guy he's going to assault our daughter, my step-daughter. That, you know, he was predating on her. I was denying it in my own mind because I was justifying everything that was going on around me. I couldn't deal with it myself. And so the only way that I chose to deal with it was to get high, and to allow the abuse to continue, because I felt like that if I let him abuse me, then I was protecting her."

Her relationship with her stepdaughter

"Jodi and I had gone through a lot of problems together. When she first came into the home she used to kick, and scream, and had bit me. She used to steal from me. She had stolen a bunch of jewelry one time of mine that was passed down to me as heirlooms, took them to school, and gave them away. But at the same time I had tried to remove myself from the situation several times, and had left the home. And Jodi had come after me, don't leave me, I'm scared, I need you, I love you. It was a very confusing mixed-up relationship. And when the child was crying out to me, I didn't know what it was that was wrong with her to begin with. I didn't know that she had been being abused. Dan had told me that she had been abused by her own mother and that she was afraid of me. It wasn't until he made that comment to me, did I begin to understand why this kid was so screwed up.

"I had been beside myself because I couldn't understand why such a small child was so violent. So, I had turned her into this little kid that clung to me for everything. Everywhere I went, she went with me. If I went to the store, she was going with me. If I did this, she was going with me. And I didn't understand why she was doing that, because she was afraid to be left alone with him. I didn't know why until the sexual assault occurred, until it started. And then I knew why she was acting like that. I believed that I was saving the child and that I was really doing her some good, when all I was doing was I was hurting her too."

The sexual abuse of her stepdaughter

"It only happened once. He started talking to me about it after the first time and he told me that he felt like that she was making advances towards him. He would just keep talking about it, and talking about it, and it was probably like six months or something like that went by. We were getting very high; we were doing all kinds of drugs intravenously. I was very addicted, very addicted. I lived the drug. We were selling it to pay the rent on our home and all of those kinds of things. I don't even know how it went on as long as it did, but it did. One night we went and we had like, I don't know a pound, a lot of drugs, a lot of drugs. This is the type of drug that keeps you awake for a very long time. We had been up for days, six days or something like that, a long time. And it was dark outside and I had had all these drugs, and a friend of ours had had the kids that day. So when the kids had been brought home I was really, really high and had been in the bathroom dividing the drugs up, and doing what it is you do to go and sell the drugs. It was probably like maybe 1:00 or 2:00 in the morning when the assault occurred. I was in the bathroom, Dan came in the bathroom, and he told me to come into the bedroom. He said that he wanted to get high. I went into the bedroom and he was in there watching pornographic movies. I stayed in the bedroom with him and we were in there getting high and arguing. He wanted me to have sex with him, and I wouldn't do it. So, he told me, go get Jodi. I told him no, I'm not going to go get her. And he said, go get her. And I said, no I'm not going to go get her. And it kept going back and forth. And then I went and got her.

"I was crying, and she was crying. I told her, I went and I woke her up and I told her to come in the room, that her dad wanted her. And she was crying, she's going 'No Mom', 'No Mom', and I was telling her, you've got to stay in here, you've got to stay in here. I told her, you need to take your pajamas off and get into bed. I told her to do it, and she did it. I went into the bathroom and told him she's in the bedroom. He went back into the bedroom and made me go into the bedroom with him. That's when he raped and molested her. I sat there watched him do it, and I didn't do nothing about it. First he went in and he was, uh, standing over her, and fondling her, and telling her to fondle him. Then he got into the bed with her. I sat there through the whole thing, the whole time. Then I was freaking out, crying, and screaming, and she was crying and screaming, and I got up and I took off, and ran out of the room. When I came back into the room she was gone. That was the only time I knew he sexually abused her. I really don't know why I stayed in the room. There was arguing going on the whole time, lots of screaming, and yelling, and hollering. And um, honestly I can't go back in my mind and tell you what made me stay in that room, but I did. The other children were home that night and about a week or so later, my son, Michael, came to me and he told me, mom, Jodi told him that her dad uh sexually…that he had sex with her. And all I could do was look at my son and tell him, that didn't happen, that didn't happen."

How she rationalized the abusive behavior

"If he asked me to get my own daughter to abuse, it wouldn't have happened. It wouldn't have happened if it was my own daughter, which means that I had no remorse over what he did to his own daughter. To me, she wasn't a human being and I didn't see her as such. Because in my mind when I allowed his child to be hurt, I was justifying that in my own mind because I felt like I was protecting my child, because if he was hurting his, then he wasn't going to be hurting mine.

"During the six months after the abuse and before my arrest, I just kept getting high. For the whole six months it was a constant conversation and a constant argument between him and I. I kept telling him, you know something is going to happen, you know that we're going to get caught, you know that we're going to go to prison, because one of those kids is going to go tell somebody. It was a constant, a constant thing, on a daily basis because I lived it every day in my head; I relived it over, and over and over again. I kept getting higher. I'm lucky that I probably didn't kill myself on drugs, because I just kept getting higher, and higher, and higher, and higher, and higher. And at one point I had tried to leave. That's when Jodi had chased me. I had loaded my kids in the car, loaded their clothes up, and was driving down the road. And I could see her in the mirror running behind us screaming. I stopped, and she begged me, don't go, don't go, I'm scared, I'm scared, so I came back, I wasn't going to run from it. I knew at the time even though I was high, that it was going to come out. It had to come out because I couldn't deal with it. And in all honesty, if one of the children hadn't told somebody, I think that it would have got to the point to where I would have. I couldn't take it. I couldn't… I was afraid to keep getting high because I was getting so high that I was at the point to where I feel like that I was probably going to OD because the amount of drugs that I was using. So in my own mind I kept thinking, well what's going to happen to all these kids if I die, and what's going to happen to my kids? I knew that it was going to come out. I'm not stupid, and I do know right from wrong, and I knew that it had to be reported. But I was afraid to go report it because I knew what was going to happen. I knew we were going to be in trouble for drugs. I know right from wrong; I don't blame this on the drugs; I don't blame it on anything. I did what I did because that's what I wanted to do because I was angry.

And it was my choice, and I made it, and it was a wrong choice. But I understand now what led me to make that poor decision."

Her other children

"The six other children were all well cared for. There was some verbal abuse as far as me being really high. Maybe the kids would come in, ask me something, or they'd be fighting and arguing, or whatever, and I'd be frustrated by it, and I would holler at them and tell them, go, go do something, and be quiet, or you're making me crazy, or whatever. I even requested to have the other children interviewed to find out if there was any abuse that I didn't know about. I kept thinking, well what happened when I wasn't there? What happened when I was at work? What happened when he was at home alone with the other kids? I kept trying to replay things in my mind, and I got frustrated with myself because there's a lot of things I don't remember because I was so high."

Her interview with the police

"I sat and talked to the investigator in my parole officer's office. I didn't even ask for an attorney. He came in the room and he goes like this. He goes, well we talked to your husband and he admitted to us everything that happened. I had already told them about what he did but I wouldn't admit to my part. He told me that, we know that you were involved. I looked at the guy and told him, I never put my hands on that child and I don't know what the hell you're talking about. And I argued with him. And then I got pissed off and I wouldn't say nothing to him at all. He kept saying to me, I know that you were in that room. And I said, I never denied that I was in that room. I'm telling you that I didn't sexually assault that child. And we got into a big ol' argument. I didn't tell him nothing about what I did because I was scared. I didn't tell him that I went and brought Jodi into the room. I didn't tell him that I told her to undress and get into the bed. I wouldn't tell him that I got up and ran out. I wouldn't tell him that I was arguing. I wouldn't tell him nothing. I was in complete denial. I was just freaking out. That was the end of the interview. He was through talking to me. He was really irritated. I was freaking out; I didn't know what to do, I didn't know, I was scared to call my family, I wouldn't seek help from anybody. And I did what I knew to do best, and I ran, I took off and I went and got high.

"I had been out of jail, and been clean, and was working, and doing everything, and then I freaked out. I thought, oh my God, I'm going to go to prison for the rest of my life. I wasn't even sentenced to prison for those check cases. I was just on probation. And I went out, and I got high and I violated my probation. As a result of that violation I came to prison. And while I was in prison this case went to court. Later on they came out and done an evaluation on me. It was during this evaluation that I admitted it. I went into court and admitted it to the judge."

Her advice for police interrogations

"I think that if he wouldn't have been like, "I know that you did it." Now keep in mind you're talking to somebody on a medicated brain and somebody that's scared. Now today it wouldn't bother me for him to tell me that, because I've been through treatment. But at the time, the way that he approached me, nobody wants a police officer to come in and tell you, I know you did this, and I know that the other person snitched on you, and we know that you did it, and we're going to get your ass. Well, your criminal behavior and your criminal thinking is to tell them, no I didn't and I don't have to tell you shit, and you can lock me up forever and I'm still not going to tell you nothing. I think that if he would have tried to talk to me as though I was the victim he would have had a better chance of getting me to talk. Maybe even if it would have been a female instead of a man, because I might not have been as intimidated. I was very abused by men. I was intimidated by the guy, and I wouldn't talk to him. I think that if it would have been a female talking to me, and at the time trying to make me feel like that I was the victim, because that's what I thought that I was. I thought I was the victim. Not her, but me, because I was the one being raped and abused, and in my mind I was the victim. Not the predator, but the victim. I think that they would have a better chance talking to me if they would talk to me from that point of a view."

Offender #8

Introduction

Offender #8[9] is a 30-year-old single white male. He has admitted to molesting approximately 30 nine-to ten-year-old boys. He had a variety of occupations working with children and was arrested at 27 years old as a result of accusations made by several nine-year-old boys he molested while he was a house parent at an orphanage.

The Interview

His abusive childhood

"It started at a very young age with my grandfather while taking a bath. He would fondle me. He also exposed himself to me, and took pictures of me in the bathroom. When I was nine he passed away, and this went on from as early as I can remember until I was nine years old when he passed away. I never told anyone about it. In fact, up until being in this

[9] Offender #8 was interviewed by Joseph P. Buckley, President of John E. Reid & Associates, Inc.

program I had a lot of denial over the fact that my grandfather had did anything wrong, because I looked up to him.

"And then at age 11 a friend of the family started molesting me. He fondled me, performed oral sex on me, and forced me to perform oral sex on him. All this was going on and another guy, the father of a friend of mine who lived right across the street, had started molesting me as well. And he sodomized me.

"The way he approached me was that I had pneumonia and I was in bed. My mother and my oldest brother had just given me an ice-cold bath to bring the fever down and then put me back in bed. He walked in my room and stuck his hand down the blankets and just started fondling me. I was very ill. I realized it was going on; I was very weak and felt like I couldn't even lift the blankets up off of me.

"My father was very abusive verbally and physically. My mom left him when I was nine years old. My mother, and this is an issue I'm really working on right now, it's a real issue for me to be able to admit to myself that there was neglect and abuse there from my mother because I always put her, just like my grandfather, I always tried to…she was the perfect parent. But she wasn't. There was no physical abuse from her, but there was definite neglect and verbal abuse."

The grooming behaviors, the setup, and progression of the sexual abuse

"At age 14 I molested two younger female cousins, which were like seven and nine, I believe, at the time. I was babysitting them and I had the nine-year-old cousin perform oral sex on me and I had the seven-year-old fondle me. I really think that I did that because I was trying to counter a bunch of the homosexual feelings that I had, you know, being three different guys. And there was a lot of confusion because I became aroused during the time that I was being molested. The one time with the female cousins I wasn't that aroused by it. It was something that I did a little bit and I was like, it's not interesting. I even went and I told my mother about it later; because I was really scared. I think it was mostly fear that I was going to get caught anyway, fear that I really didn't understand what was going on. I was having these feelings and yet here was two girls and I didn't have any arousal to what they were doing to me and it was just very confusing. All of my victims from that point on have been boys. My highest arousal is to boys between the ages of eight and eleven years old. I don't know why. Older kids just don't have the same arousal level, it's there, but it's not as high.

"I was between 21 and 22 when I started molesting boys. It started after I was out of the Army. The only sexual activity I had in the Army was with a prostitute. My sergeant had found out that basically I was a virgin, and you can't have that in the company, so he went out and he bought me a prostitute. I was like 17 or 18 at the time.

"My first male victim was when I was 21. It was a friend of my mother and stepfather's, acquaintances. I was watching them, they had come over. Two young boys had come over and stayed the night at my house. There were a seven- and a nine-year-old boy. I molested the nine-year-old. I started fondling him, and I took him into my bedroom and performed oral sex on him. The seven-year-old was out watching TV. I never had any real contact with these children after that.

"I didn't molest another child for a couple of years. There was what I would call covert abuse during that time. I was peeping. If I was wrestling with a child, I would let my hand brush across them through their clothing. So during that time there was covert abuse. But as far as the actual molesting, it would have been a couple years later. It was a 13-year-old boy who I talked into masturbating in front of me while I masturbated in front of him. His grandmother lived across the street from me. It happened once in his house and once in mine. I told him this is just between you and I; this is not something we need to talk about.

"I guess it was like another year and a half before I chose my next victim. I was working with his father and his father had invited me over to their house. I started spending a lot of time around there. His father actually started making passes at me. And, basically, his father apparently had seen the way I was looking at his son; he also is in prison right now for child molestation, so he was obviously able to pick up on some of my actions. And he basically offered his son to me to molest if I would have sexual acts with him. It happened very gradually. I would spend the night and I would be allowed to sleep in the son's bed. His son would have been eight or nine at the time that this began. It was kind of, you know, being arranged so I would sleep in the same bed as he was. But later after I had known him for about six to eight months he left his wife. When his son would come over to visit it was very clear that… I mean, it was even talked about that I could do such and such to his son, perform oral sex on him or whatever if I would let him perform oral sex on me. I also had taken a couple pictures of him, so that when he wasn't there that I could look at them and fantasize about molesting him.

"This whole situation was kind of odd because I had found out later that the mother had also been molesting the child from a very young age. So, he had neither one of his parents he could go tell or talk to. He knew his father knew what was going on, and his mother was basically doing the same thing to him.

"This went on for about three years on and off. In fact, it went up to like six to eight months that I didn't see him at all because his mother had actually found out that I was molesting him. She had threatened to turn me in. That's how I found out that she had been molesting him, because the boy's father had told her; well I was there if you say anything about what he is doing, then I will tell what you have been doing.

"I made a profession out of working with children. That put me in a position where I was very close to them, and also in a position where both the adults around me and the children trusted me with the kids. I started out as a Scout leader, volunteering in a child-care center, and I later became employed with that center. I was a school bus driver as well as volunteering in the libraries of this parochial school. Then I got a job at the orphanage for young boys. I didn't molest any of the children at the day care because they were all below the actual age that I was interested in. I did fantasize about them though.

"While I worked as a bus driver there was a lot of covert abuse. I was also at a library, volunteering in the library, so I would walk down into the boys' bathroom; and while I was not touching them, I certainly was walking up to the urinal or whatever and watching them. Also, wrestling, and playing, and touching them on the outside of their clothing; something that a child doesn't really think a lot of if it's real quick. It was an accident, you know, as you're wrestling with them and your hand just happens to brush across them. It just happens. It was very purposely, obviously. So there was a lot of that type of abuse. Now there was some that I had invited over to my house that actually came over to my house, and I peeped on them while they were taking baths. There was one who I knew from the time he was 13 to the time he was 15, and at 15 years old I molested him. I performed oral sex on him, I masturbated him, and I had him perform oral sex on me.

"I would meet the kids one way or the other; it would be either through the parents, or from my job. A lot of it was just knowing their parents, getting to know their parents, then offering to take their child to the park, to a movie, take them roller skating, something that they would enjoy. Then I would get to know the child to gain their trust. Play games with them and do things that they would enjoy doing, just gain their trust. Once I had their trust I would slowly then move in, rubbing their back, going down touching their buttocks, rubbing their chest and letting my hand run down across their penis, and just gradually move up. At the same time I would be talking to them, does this feel good? And this is a lot of my justification to make me feel that it was okay; I would ask them does this feel good, do you like this? At the same time, telling the children that if they told anyone that then they would never be able to see me again, that I wouldn't be able to be their friend anymore. I put it off on them by telling them that if they told, they're going to lose this person that's giving them attention. I would say every one of my victims that was what I used was attention. They were not getting it somewhere else and they were getting it from me. I was giving them it, obviously in a negative way, but they felt they were getting some type of attention.

"I would initially engage in a lot of covert abuse to…I guess I was I feeling the victim out. I was getting aroused by it; and at the same time I wanted to see what the child's reaction was to it. If they didn't say anything about my hand brushing across them through their clothing, next time it would be a little longer, and next time it would be a little longer. Some victims it would not go any further, maybe because of their reaction or maybe simply because the opportunity wasn't there as far as them coming over and me being alone with them or whatever. But I would do this in front of dozens of people while wrestling with them and playing and stuff. A lot of the covert abuse would be done right in front of other people. I think they thought he accidentally touched me. It must have been an accident, mom, dad, whoever, is sitting right here. So, when I would get them alone and touch them, they were confused. Because there was nothing said when I touched them in front of mom, so it must be ok. But mom wasn't really paying attention; I was wrestling with him, you know, it wasn't like I just reached out and grabbed him. I was wrestling and it was just something that happened.

"Sometimes I would buy the child gifts. Especially if the child is from a low-income home, family where there's not a lot of money, gifts mean a lot to them as far as they know if they tell, then the gifts are going to stop and they're not going to get the toys, the new pair of jeans that they really wanted, or the shoes. At the same time using that and buying gifts, able to buy clothing that I actually wanted to see the children wear. I would buy them clothes that I thought were more exciting to see them in or that were more accessible. Like sweats, shorts, definitely more accessible to molest them; there were no zippers and buttons that had to be undone. At the same time, Spandex or biker shorts were more arousing because of the tight fit. I bought a number of my victims colored underwear, the fashionable style underwear so that I could see them in those.

"I never picked up a stranger off the street to molest. I felt safer with someone I knew because I used love as a weapon. I loved them. And with all of my victims, that was something that they were looking for was love. And so, I felt safer doing it that way; whereas to go out and solicit to pick up a child that doesn't know me, they're not going to have that fear of telling on me, that they're going to lose that love.

"If a child ever resisted me I would just back way off. I would move in real gradually, like rubbing their back. That way it would be very easy for me to say that my hand slipped or I'm sorry. And sort of wrestling and let my hand rub across the private areas, then I could say that it was an accident. I was moving slowly. If they were comfortable with me touching them there when we were wrestling, then that way I could see. And if the child put up any resistance, then I would back off because I would just simply go find another victim.

"Most of the molesting took place at my house. Now with the child that his father knew I was molesting him, it happened in his house as well. But most generally it was my house. Most generally what I would do is I would get the children to come over and spend the night at my house. And do it at my house. You see I was working with the kids professionally and had the trust of the parents. I was working at the day care and then I was driving a school bus. Then after I left the orphanage I started working at a children's shelter, and I was a Scout leader. So I was working with the children, so in that way I used the parents as well to gain their trust. What that does then is it takes the whole support system away from the child; well, Mom and Dad says he's a good person; Mom and Dad likes him, or Mom. Most of my victims were from single-parent homes. Mom says he's a good person so, you know, he must be a good person. And then I think a lot of the victims then questioned, it must be me because everyone around me is saying he's a good person.

"Things were a little different when I had the job as a house parent caring for 8- to 10-year-old boys at the orphanage. I was living in the house. There were about 200 to 300 children in the orphanage but only about ten in my house. Every one of them were victims of covert abuse as far as walking down and seeing them in the shower, peeping on them and stuff. I molested four of the victims in my hall, and I molested six other children that were not in my hall. I was in charge of these boys 24 hours a day, 7 days a week. I lived with them. So the opportunity was always there. That was the reason I took the job, because I was there with them 24 hours a day, 7 days a week. I didn't have to go look for victims. I was living there."

Why he sexually molests children

"I'm really still working on that. I don't know that I'll ever know the exact reasons why. I really don't know why. I know that's what I was aroused to, I know that it's related to my being abused, but at the same time I cannot say that…I cannot blame that because as an adult I knew it was wrong. I felt more comfortable around kids. I mean, the kids weren't judging how I was. The kids weren't judging who I was. I felt cared about. There's a lot of fear of entering any relationship with adults, and so with children it was easier because they weren't judging me.

"After molesting them I would have a fear of being caught; I would feel guilt and shame. I would tell myself I'm never going to do it again; and yet, sometimes even within the same day I would be doing it again. I would feel guilt and shame but then later I would start feeling lonely, feeling sexually aroused, feeling unloved, un-cared-about. I felt I was getting that love from the children. After the abuse I would just act normal, like it never happened. After I went through the justifications, then I would be acting like nothing happened, acting like the good guy. So it was just acting like it never happened."

How he manipulated his victims and rationalized his abusive behavior

"I rationalized it by telling myself that they wanted to do it, that I wasn't hurting them because there was no physical pain. I used the fact that I did not sodomize any of my victims. There was no physical pain so I wasn't hurting them. I loved them, they loved me. I was just telling myself it was love, and at the same time that I wasn't harming them because there was no physical pain. At the time I thought I loved them. I told myself, anyway, that I loved them and I cared about them. But actually, it was all for me. Most of my victims prior to the orphanage I don't even remember their names. So, obviously, if you care about a person, if you love a person, you're not going to forget their name. Most of my victims I do not even remember their names. So I think that more than anything else is a clear message to me that I didn't care about them at all, and I didn't love them, because now I don't even remember their names.

"I was telling myself it was mutual consent. I used that by asking them, can I do this? Do you want to do this? And if they said no, I wouldn't do it. I would simply find a victim that would say yes. I know there's no such thing as mutual consent when it's a child. They're not able to give consent. But at the same time I told myself it was mutual consent. They knew that the only way they were going to get my attention, my 'love' as I called it, was if they allowed me to do these things to them. So, whether they were giving consent, which again they can't give consent, but whether they were saying yes because they wanted to have these sexual acts, I do not believe now. At the time that's what I as telling myself. But it was just the attention that they were wanting, and the only way they were going to get the attention was if I got what I wanted."

His preferred victim

"They had to be white; I was not sexually aroused by any children other than white children, introverted, and lonely. I think as a child molester I have like a sixth sense. I look at a child and I automatically start honing in on, is he lonely? Is he introverted? Does he have a low self-esteem, already feeling not real outgoing, not hanging around with lots of other kids, not having lots of friends, looking for their friend? I would look for kids who either came from single-parent homes or homes that I knew that the father just wasn't there for the kids. He may live there, but that doesn't mean he was there for the kids, because they're looking for a male role model, a male image, attention from an adult male. Where a child that has a father who is spending a lot of time with him, that does take him places and pays attention to him, it's not as easy to set them up because they're getting that attention, they're not looking for that attention already from an adult male.

"If there was any resistance really I would just back off because I knew that I could always find another victim. It wasn't worth getting caught to physically force the child. So if the child resisted, I would just simply back off. At the same time, then, I would just ignore that child. I would no longer take that child places, I would no longer be around that child, I would just simply back off and find another victim."

His description of common characteristics of child molesters

"I think we see it in other people more so than someone who is not another child molester. There's been throughout my life, adult life, there's been a number of people I've looked at and pretty much known that they are a child molester. And then in a couple of cases they were later arrested and it was confirmed. So I think that there are things that we see. I know my own actions, so when I see those exact same actions in someone else, it really gives me a clear indication that, well, they may be a molester. Like if they're spending all their time hanging around kids and not adults. A lot of people work with kids and are doing it for healthy reasons. But when there's no adult relationships, they're not spending any time with adults, all their time is focused on spending with kids; when they're focused on being alone with kids; when they're buying kids gifts, taking kids lots of places; spending money on them, lots of money. Also, I think it's just in the way that they…I know one of the things that he noticed in me was just simply the way I was looking at his son. I think that I have noticed that in other people as well, just the way that they're focused and looking.

"To use the example of Little League coaches, being a coach there's going to be a number of kids around. If that person starts singling a child out and wanting to spend lots of time *alone* with that child where they're not with the rest of the team, then I would…not saying that he is, but I would definitely be very careful. If he starts buying gifts for the child I would be very careful."

His interview with the police

"I had left the orphanage and went back to live in Indiana. I had been there for six months before they found out about what I was doing at the orphanage, and I was arrested. That's basically when it stopped. They found out what I was doing because this other guy who was molesting the children at the orphanage turned me in. He later got caught and arrested himself. The detective told me that the reason he turned me in was to build a trust at the orphanage. You know, he turned in a child molester; certainly he must be a trustworthy person.

"When I was questioned by the police I denied everything. I denied it right up to the time that I came in this program. In fact, I'm smiling because I was thinking of the first time that I was interviewed to come into the program. I sat there and asked to come into the program and yet denied that I had ever done it. So even though I was saying I wanted to join the program, I was saying I had never done it. Well, why do you need the program?

"The reason I didn't admit it to the police was the fear of going to prison, the fear of what people would think; oh, he's a child molester. Just the reaction and being locked up. I know one thing that the officer who interviewed me did that kind of tripped me up on my lies; which was, he had said something about not hurting them. Well my first snap-back was, well you know, if I did these things, I must be hurting them. And I think he clearly knew from the very first time he talked to me that I was guilty and that I had done it. It was just the way I answered the questions, the way I was trying to go around. Well, yeah I had to give them a bath, that was my job; things like that."

His comments on whether he would offend again

"I know that I always have to be afraid that there's that possibility. If I ever come to a point that I'm not afraid of re-offending, then that's when I would be the closest to being offending. Because I know who I am, and I know I'm a child molester, and I know what I've done in the past. So I know that if I'm not very careful not to enter the high-risk situations, not to put myself and a child in those dangerous situations, that there is a very high possibility that I would re-offend. So, for me, it's knowing that I'm…there is no cure. It's just like being an alcoholic. If you're an alcoholic, you're always an alcoholic but you never have to take another drink. I'll always be a child molester, but I never have to victimize another child. Because as I said, at any point I thought, well I don't have to worry about it, I'm never going to re-offend. Then that's when I would be probably the closest to re-offending because my guard is down and I'm not paying attention."

His warning to parents

"I think one very important thing is to let their kids know there are just people out there that will hurt them, to let them know that they can come to them at anytime and talk to them about anything; and that if something like this was to happen, it's not their fault. Because, that's one of the main things that I know I used was that by asking the children, does this feel good, do you like this? then I was putting it off on them so that they would feel, you know, I wanted this, it's my fault. So let the children know it is not their fault. And basically let the children know that they can come and talk to them about anything. Letting the child know that they have the right to say 'no.' Too often kids are told that they have to obey adults. So kids sometimes don't know that they have the right to say 'no' and that this is their body and they have a right. I think a lot of it is in the parents and the schools having sessions where they actually teach the children that they do have a right to say 'no' and to go tell.

"I think that saying at any point that the child could have protected themselves is putting some blame on them; obviously, the child is not to blame at all. To me, there's no responsibility there on the child at all where they could have and couldn't have. That's one of the important things. Once a parent or any adult realizes that a child has been molested, I know I used to work with children, you hear so often, 'Why didn't you tell sooner?' Or, 'I was just near the room, why didn't you scream?' I think that only adds to the guilt and the shame feelings that the kids have. So it's very important that the adults who, once they recognize their child has been a victim, that they are very careful in how they treat them or question them.

"If a child's behavior changes erratically from good grades to bad grades, or all of the sudden they're more withdrawn, they never wet the bed and now they've started wetting the bed. It doesn't say that they have been molested, but these are things that definitely mean something's wrong and that the parent should be talking to the kid. If an adult is buying this child gifts or if this child is coming up with money and/or items that their parents can't explain where they're coming from. Again, parents need to start asking their children and keeping an eye on it. If their kid is more interested in spending time with this one particular adult than anyone else, definitely again doesn't mean something's happening, but start asking questions."

Part 2

Practical Guidelines for Identifying, Interviewing and Interrogating Child Abuse Offenders

Chapter 2

Introduction

Part One of this book offered the reader a glimpse into the minds of eight child abuse offenders whose backgrounds and life circumstances provide enough differentiation to act as a vehicle to illustrate the interviewing and interrogation techniques that will be developed in Part Two. Our many years of experience interviewing child abuse offenders at John E. Reid & Associates, Inc. have led to the development of interviewing and interrogation techniques that have proven to be effective in identifying offenders and eliciting the truth from them. Part Two will discuss the type of information investigators need to develop in the interview, the questions investigators should ask to develop that information, and how investigators can use that information to identify the offender and develop an interrogation strategy.

The success of an investigative interview or interrogation of a child abuse offender begins with the attitude and preparation of the investigator. Investigators should approach the interview with a nonjudgmental attitude and an understanding of human nature. This can be particularly challenging in child abuse investigations. In spite of the investigator's personal feelings, it is important that the investigator treat every subject with decency and respect.

The subsequent chapters in Part Two are designed to help investigators prepare for the interview and interrogation. Chapter 3 will discuss the importance of the interview environment and identify the common behavioral patterns, attitudes, and characteristics of individuals who are inclined to physically or sexually abuse a child. Chapter 4 will discuss interviewing techniques to include evaluating the subject's alibi, the use of investigative questions and the use of behavior provoking questions. Chapter 5 will discuss the interrogation techniques that investigators can employ to elicit the truth from the offender to include an overview of the Reid Nine Steps® of interrogation, and suggestions for theme development[10] for child abuse investigations.

The difference between the interview and the interrogation

First, it is important to understand the difference between the interview and the interrogation. Most investigators have a tendency to combine questioning a subject with challenges to the subject's statements. They do not distinguish the interview from the interrogation and use the words interview and interrogation interchangeably. Failure to distinguish between these two procedures hampers the investigator's ability to develop

---

[10] Theme development is step two of the Reid Nine Steps of Interrogation. It is a monologue whereby the interrogator offers the offender psychological justifications to minimize in the offenders mind the seriousness of the abusive behavior.

rapport with the subject and limits the amount of information available for the development of a successful interrogation strategy.

The Interview

The most distinct characteristic of the interview is that it is *non-accusatory*. Investigators should conduct a non-accusatory interview whether there is credible evidence identifying the guilty offender or the identity of the offender is uncertain. The information developed in the interview will help determine if the subject manifests any of the common behavioral patterns or characteristics consistent with an individual who is inclined to abuse a child. This not only plays a critical role in determining the truthfulness of the subject but also in the development of a successful interrogation strategy. Therefore it is important to encourage the subject to do most of the talking during the interview. To facilitate this, the interviewer should have a series of questions prepared in advance. The questions should be designed to elicit information regarding the subject's possible involvement in the abusive behavior. Interviewers should take written notes during the interview even if the interview is being electronically recorded. Taking written notes allows the interviewer to control the pace of the interview and insures an accurate record of the subject's statements in the event the electronic equipment fails. Investigators should separate each question with a pause of silence rather than asking them in a rapid-fire manner. The pause of silence will allow the deceptive person to consider their deceptive response to the investigator's question which will increase their level of anxiety. The deceptive subject is more apt to display behavior symptoms of deception as their anxiety level increases. On the other hand, a rapid-fire questioning approach may confuse the truthful subject.

The Interrogation

For most people, the word interrogation conjures up an image of a subject sitting under a bright light with the interrogator looming over them in a less than sympathetic manner. This is why investigators avoid the use of the word interrogation. Instead they refer to their interrogation as an interview or conversation. The most distinctive characteristic of the interrogation is that it is accusatory. Even though it is accusatory the investigator should project a sympathetic or empathetic attitude toward the subject throughout the procedure. The investigator should dominate the conversation and offer rationalizations or psychological justifications that will serve to minimize the moral seriousness of the offense in the mind of the offender. These rationalizations should reflect the offenders pre-existing pattern of thought and be presented in the form of a monologue. This approach is designed to create an environment where the subject feels comfortable telling the truth. The investigator must be reasonably sure of the offender's guilt before subjecting him to an interrogation. Unlike the interview, the investigator does not want to conduct an interrogation unless he has completed a thorough investigation and has adequate information about the offense, victim and offender to develop an interrogation strategy. To enhance the element of privacy in the interrogation, the investigator should avoid taking any notes until the subject admits his guilt, at which time the investigator will take a written or electronically recorded statement from the subject. Throughout the interrogation the investigator should project an attitude that the only reason he is talking to the subject is to determine the circumstance under which the abuse occurred.

Most child protection workers (CPW) have experience interviewing alleged offenders but few have experience interrogating offenders. It is the police detective who normally conducts the interrogation. However, the CPW can still play an important role in this phase of the investigation. The detective conducting the interrogation may benefit from the knowledge the CPW has developed through their interviews with family members, teachers, neighbors and others who may have provided child protection services with information regarding the alleged abuse. Therefore, it is important that CPW not only have a clear understanding of the interview phase of the process but also of the interrogation phase of the investigation. Moreover, there may be times when the CPW must confront the alleged offender themselves.

Chapter 3

Preparation Prior To The Interview

The Importance of the Interview Environment

The interview environment plays a significant role in an interviewer's ability to evaluate truthfulness and solicit information from an alleged offender. The ideal environment to conduct an investigative interview is one that is *private* and *free of distractions*. There are three types of environments available to conduct interviews or interrogations - each has its advantages and disadvantages. The interview can be conducted in an environment that is supportive to the subject (i.e. their home), an environment that is supportive to the interviewer (i.e. the investigator's office), or a neutral environment that is not particularly supportive to either (i.e. a restaurant / neutral office site).

Privacy

The information the investigator is trying to solicit from an alleged offender or witness in child abuse investigations is very sensitive and the subject may not be willing to reveal this secret information in an environment where he fears others may be listening. Ideally the interviewer should be the only one in the interview room with the subject and avoid having any barriers separating him from the subject, such as a table or desk, as illustrated in Figure 3-1. This will allow the interviewer to develop a rapport and a level of trust with the offender. If a third person is in the room as an observer the subject may be reluctant to disclose sensitive information. Consider the following case example.

Case Example

> During one of my training programs I was asked to review a videotape of an interrogation of a father who sexually assaulted his 13-year-old daughter. The father was being questioned by a detective while a child protection worker, who had interviewed the victim, sat in the room off to the side observing. The father denied the allegations. During the interrogation the detective presented a variety of rationalizations for the father's abusive behavior but was unsuccessful eliciting the truth from him. The offender continued to deny ever sexually touching his daughter. Throughout the interrogation the offender avoided making eye contact with the CPW. A point was reached in the interrogation where it was evident that the offender was not going to admit the abuse at this time. He was released and asked to return a few days later. After reviewing the interrogation it was agreed that the offender was inhibited by the presence of the CPW. Therefore the CPW agreed to observe the subsequent interrogation from an

observation room. The offender returned as scheduled and the detective conducted this interrogation alone. He presented the same type of monologue as he did in the earlier interrogation only this time the effect was the complete opposite. After developing a thirty-minute monologue the offender admitted sexually touching his daughter.

Certain situations may necessitate the presence of a third person or witness to be in the room with the investigator and the subject. When a male investigator is interviewing a female subject of questionable character it may be advantageous to have another female present to discourage potential false allegations of impropriety. In circumstances where the presence of a third person is unavoidable and an observation room is not available, the investigator should seat the third person in the back of and to the side of the subject as illustrated in Figure 3-2. This seating arrangement will minimize the presence of the third person.

Figure 3-1 Interview room arrangement with subject and interviewer

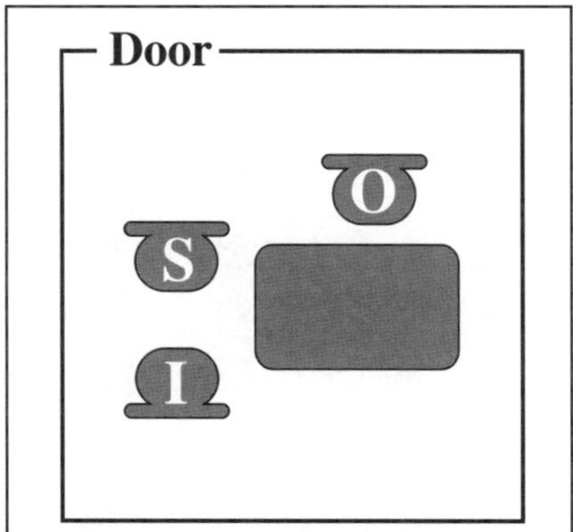

Figure 3-2 Interview room arrangement with observer

Distractions

Investigators should take the time to reduce distractions as much as possible in the interview room to enhance the reliability of behavior symptom analysis. Cell phones and office phones should be turned off, a "do not disturb" notice should be placed on the outside of the door, indicating an interview is in progress. The desk or table in the room should be cleared of clutter and the subject's chair should not face an outside window or a window to the inner office. The investigator should avoid having anything draw the subject's attention away from the investigator's questions. The more distractions there are in the interview environment the more difficult it will be to assess the offender's behavior.

The subject's supportive environment

In child abuse investigations, interviewing the alleged offender in their home environment will provide the interviewer an opportunity to evaluate the alleged offender's style of living, the safety and cleanliness of the home, and identify all individuals who reside there. In physical abuse investigations a home visit will also provide the CPW an opportunity to view and even photograph the area in the home where the injury allegedly occurred, i.e. the changing table the infant allegedly fell from, or the objects or toys the child allegedly fell on, causing their injuries. This may help establish the credibility of the allegation.

The disadvantage of interviewing in the subject's supportive environment is that the interviewer gives up control over distractions and privacy. The subject may be distracted during the interview because of the household responsibilities they have with their family. The subject will also have the freedom of removing himself from the interview if his tension level is getting difficult for him to tolerate. In an effort to reduce the level of anxiety produced by the interview the subject may excuse himself to check on his children or to turn off the oven.

The investigator's supportive environment

Interviewing the subject in the investigator's supportive environment will give the investigator control over the setup of the room, the privacy element, and the distractions. This supportive environment will enhance the investigator's ability to accurately assess the subject's behavior displayed during the interview. If the subject is deceptive, there is a stronger likelihood of successfully eliciting an admission of guilt during the interrogation in this environment.

The room should suggest a professional atmosphere that is designed for this purpose. The chairs should be reasonably comfortable and set approximately four to five feet apart without any barriers, such as a table or desk, between the interviewer and subject. The distance between the chairs will show a respect for personal space. If the interviewer sits too close (two to three feet) to the subject it may cause the subject to push their chair back or put up physical barriers such as crossing their arms or legs. Furthermore, interviewing across a desk or table will interfere with the investigator's ability to observe the subject's behavior. The temperature in the room should be comfortable and the lighting should be bright enough to see the subject's nonverbal behavior during the interview but not so bright as to be shining in the subject's eyes.

The disadvantage of interviewing or interrogating in an environment that is supportive to the investigator is that the subject may refuse to voluntarily come in for questioning or he may only agree to an interview if his attorney is present. Another consideration is that the subject may not have transportation to get to the facility or may have to take public transportation which can be time consuming and inconvenient.

Preparing for the Interview: Areas of Interest in Child Abuse Investigations

The investigator should develop the following areas of information during an interview of an alleged offender of either sexual or physical abuse and be able to answer the following questions at the conclusion of the interview:

1. Does the alleged offender engage in any of the *common behavioral patterns or display any of the personality characteristics* that are consistent with an individual who has the *propensity* to abuse a child?
2. Does the alleged offender try to *minimize* the seriousness of the abuse or try to *rationalize* the abusive behavior?
3. What circumstances were present that may have *precipitated* or contributed to the subject's decision to abuse the child?
4. What is the alleged offender's *relationship with the victim*? What is the alleged offender's perception of the victim?

5. Did the alleged offender engage in *verbal or non-verbal behavior symptoms* that are indicative of truth or deception?

The answers to these questions will help determine the truthfulness of the alleged offender and provide the information necessary for the development of a successful interrogation strategy for those offenders who are guilty of abusing the child.

Child Sexual Offenders

Sexual abuse is any misuse of a child for sexual pleasure or gratification, not limited to but including: non-touching sexual abuse such as indecent exposure, showing children pornographic material or deliberately exposing a child to sexual acts; touching sexual offenses such as fondling, making a child touch another person's sexual organ, any penetration of a child's vagina or anus by an object that doesn't have a medical purpose; sexual exploitation offenses such as using a child for the purposes of prostitution, or using a child to film, photograph or model pornography.

Common Behavior Patterns and Characteristics

It is difficult to develop a classification or list of characteristics that will consistently identify a sexual offender. Child molesters present a façade making them indistinguishable from other people. There is no psychological profile of the typical child molester or psychological test that has been consistently effective identifying child molesters.[11] Researchers have tried to identify correlations between race, religion, intelligence, education, occupation, or socioeconomic status to identify child molesters only to find that none of these characteristics distinguish perpetrators from non- perpetrators.[12] Offenders themselves recognize their ability to blend in with the general population as illustrated in the comments of Offender #1:

> *"I think anybody that is in any kind of a predatory mode is going to put out a socially acceptable aura about them. The great fallacy that sex offenders are hiding in bushes, and lurking in trees and this kind of stuff is a crock... we're the guy who lives next door. We're the guy that's coaching your kid's baseball team; we're the priest at the church. Mentally, if we're working like we*

---

[11] Becker J. V., & Coleman E. M. (1988). "Incest". In V. B. Van Hasselt, R. L. Morrison , A. S. Bellack, & M. Hersen (Eds.), *Handbook of family violence* (pp. 187-205). New York: Plenum Press. Knight R. A., Rosenberg R., & Schneider B. A. (1985). *Classification of sexual offenders; perspectives, methods, and validation.*; Burgess A. W. (Ed.), *Rape and sexual assault* (pp. 222-293). New York: Garland Publications: Crewdson J. (1988). *By silence betrayed: Sexual abuse of children in America*. Boston: Little, Brown.

[12] Erickson, W. D., Luxenberg, M. G., Walbek, N. H., and Seely, R. K. (1987). Frequency of MMPI two-point code types among sex offenders. J. Consult. Clin. Psychol. 55: 566-570: Atwood R., & Howell R. (1971). Pupillometric and personality test scores of female aggressing pedophiliacs and normals. *Psychonomic Science*, 22, 115-116: McCreary C. P. (1975). Personality differences among child molesters. *Journal of Personality Assessment*, 39, 6, 591-593: Groth A. N., Hobson W. F., & Gary T. S. (1982). "The child molester: Clinical observations"; Conte J. & Shore D. A. (Eds.), *Social Work and Child Sexual Abuse* (pp.129-144). New York: Haworth.

should, even though we're being deviant, we all want to put out that front that says, this is a nice guy. This is, you know, this is a good guy and he wouldn't do this kind of thing."

Researchers have also made an attempt to place sexual offenders into classifications such as Fixed vs Regressed offenders, Situational vs Preferential offenders, Incestuous vs Non-incestuous offenders, or Socially competent vs Socially incompetent offenders.[13] However, none of these classifications alone capture the vast array of individual characteristics and social circumstances of all sexual offenders. There are, however, a number of personality characteristics, and patterns of behavior that have been associated with sexual offenders.[14] This list of common characteristics and behavioral patterns can assist the investigator in the development of interview questions designed to elicit information that will serve to identify whether an alleged offender has any of the characteristics or behavioral patterns that have been identified as consistent with someone who is more inclined to sexually abuse a child.

---

[13] Groth N. A. (1982). The incest offender. In S. M. Sgroi (Ed.), *Handbook of clinical intervention in child sexual abuse*. Lexington, MA: Lexington Books. Knight R. A., Carter D. L., U+ 0026 R. A. Prentky (1989). "A system for the classification of child molesters: Reliability and application". *Journal of Interpersonal Violence, 4*, 3-23.

[14] These characteristics and behavioral patterns are based on observations made by the staff of John E. Reid & Associates, Inc from interviews of child abuse offenders and research conducted in the field. See list of resources in appendix.

Characteristics of Sexual Offenders

- poor impulse control
- emotionally immature
- self-centered
- hypersensitive
- 30-50% suffer from alcoholism
- sexually promiscuous
- unable to control their sexual urges
- experience sexual obsessions and compulsions
- shy
- poor social skills
- low self-esteem
- skilled manipulators
- fearful and distrustful of adults
- narcissistic or egocentric
- lack a sense of power and control in their lives
- poor relationship with their parents
- inadequate coping skills
- abused themselves as children
- unstable marriages
- minor criminal histories
- find children sexually arousing
- experience sexual anxiety or are sexually frustrated
- difficulty developing intimate adult relationships

Physical Characteristics of Sexual Offenders

- 90% are male
- 71% of sexual offenders are younger than 35 years of age
- the average age of a sexual offender is 31 years old

Behavioral Patterns of Sexual Offenders

- frequent locations where children are
- astute at reading the cues that signal the vulnerability of a victim
- skillful at disarming and controlling their victims
- willing to exploit children's trust to satisfy their own needs
- the abuse is progressive in nature
- fantasize prior to abusing
- give children money and gifts routinely
- experience a high level of stress in their lives prior to abusing
- may perceive women as larger than life and possess more social power and control than men

Characteristics of Juvenile Sexual Offenders[15]

- emotionally immature
- low self esteem
- experience poor emotional control
- identify with younger children

---

[15] These characteristics of juvenile sexual offenders reflect our observations and those of several experts in the field. Perry, G., & Orchard, J. (1992). Assessment and treatment of adolescent sex offenders. Sarasota, FL: Professional Resource Press.; Breer, W. (1987). The adolescent molester. Springfield, IL: Charles C. Thomas. Davis, G. E., & Leitenberg, H. (1987). Adolescent sex offenders. Psychological Bulletin, 101, 417-427.

- mother was unaffectionate, demanding, intrusive, and belittling
- father was emotionally distant, indifferent, and uninvolved, abusive
- have a history of loneliness, school problems, antisocial behavior
- there is usually a progression of offenses from peeping – indecent exposure – solicitation
- have sexual fantasies about the molestation
- sex offenses are often motivated by a need for recognition, approval and power
- select victims younger than themselves they can control
- have a manipulative personal style
- have marginal social development
- avoid positive interactions with opposite sex peers

Unfortunately there is no formula or equation available that will identify someone as a sexual offender. Some sexual offenders may have several of the listed characteristics while others may only exhibit a few of these characteristics. In addition to these common characteristics investigators should try to identify whether the subject has engaged in the six behavioral patterns that are consistent with sexual offenders. Those patterns of behavior are as follows:

1. Victim selection
2. Setting up the opportunity to abuse
3. Isolating the victim
4. Grooming the victim

5. Manipulating the victim

6. Rationalizing their abusive behavior

Victim selection

Offenders are very astute at reading the cues that signal the vulnerability of a victim. This ability plays a critical factor in victim selection. Research has shown that as many as 49% of offenders looked for children who appeared to have low self-esteem or a lack of self- confidence.[16]

Offender #8 describes his victim selection.

> *"I would look for kids who either came from single-parent homes or that I knew that the father just wasn't there for the kids. He may live there, but that doesn't mean he was there for the kids, because they're looking for a male role model, a male image, attention from an adult male. Where a child that has a father who is spending a lot of time with him, that does take him places and pays attention to him; it's not as easy to set them up because they're getting that attention, they're not looking for that attention already from an adult male... the only way they were going to get my attention, my 'love' as I called it, was if they allowed me to do these things to them.*
>
> *"At the time I thought I loved them. I told myself, anyway, that I loved them and I cared about them. But actually, it was all*

---

[16] Elliot, M., Browne, K., & Kilcoyne, J. (1995). Child sexual abuse prevention: What offenders tell us. Child Abuse and Neglect, 19, 579-594.

> *for me. Most of my victims prior to the orphanage I don't even remember their names. So obviously if you care about a person, if you love a person, you're not going to forget their names...So I think that more than anything else is a clear message to me that I didn't care about them at all, and I didn't love them, because now I don't even remember their names."*

Some offenders look for weaknesses in the child's personality or life circumstances. For example, a child who is shy or introverted and does not have a lot of friends, or comes from a single-parent family and is not getting very much attention at home. Offenders familiarize themselves with the video games, TV shows, music, books, and movies the child is interested in to enhance their ability to connect with the child at their level. They will make the child feel as though they are very interested in the same things and try to make them feel special or important because this adult is showing them so much attention. Children love attention, as one offender explains:

> *"We make it known to the child that we are totally interested in them over and above their parents, siblings, or other friends. Children love attention and can become easy prey."*

Characteristics offenders look for in victims[17]

- A child who is a lonely, quiet, or passive
- A child who is looking for attention
- A child from a single-parent family
- A child who has no siblings at home so there is no one for them to tell
- A child who has already been sexually abused because they are viewed as "damaged goods"
- A child who comes from a dysfunctional family where there is physical abuse or substance abuse, because the child will have no one to go to for support
- Girls who appear to be sexually active
- A child whose credibility is in question
- Boys who did not have a good relationship with their father or are having family difficulties
- Children who seemed affectionate
- Unsupervised girls in public places such as in a toy store, or toy department of a store, playgrounds, parks, neighborhoods, church.

---

[17] Ward, T. (1999) Competency and Deficit Models in the Understanding and Treatment of Sexual Offenders. The Journal of Sex Research. Volume: 36. Issue: 3. Page Number: 298: Elliot, M., Browne, K., & Kilcoyne, J. (1995). Child sexual abuse prevention: What offenders tell us: Budin, L. E., & Johnson, C. F. (1989). Sex abuse prevention programs: Offenders' attitudes about their efficacy. Child Abuse and Neglect, 13, 77-87: Conte, J. R., Wolf, S., & Smith, T. (1989). What sexual offenders tell us about prevention strategies. Child Abuse and Neglect, 13, 293-301: Miltenberger, Raymond G. & Roberts, Jennifer A. (1999) Emerging Issues in the Research on Child Sexual Abuse Prevention. Journal Title: Education & Treatment of Children. Volume: 22. Issue: 1. Page Number: 84.

- A child with low self esteem, and self-confidence

Offender #1 comments on the characteristics he looked for in his victims:

"Then after I had them all groomed, or while I was grooming them, I'd be picking out the ones that might be vulnerable. By acting like I was interested in them, cared about them, got me information about who's living with grandma that's blind and deaf, who's living on Welfare or whatever. Who is the only kid in the house? Which one is a single child, because sometimes sisters will talk. Or, brothers and sisters will talk. If I had a single child living in a home with a single parent, who was like on the dole and spending it on beer. Or a single parent who's working three jobs trying to get the bills met, then this kid didn't get much time at home. I knew the kid was vulnerable. I would single out kids that were being ignored. If they're working at their desk, and they're sitting there, and they're bent over working, and a key on a chain falls out from around their neck; I'll ask them, what's that to? Do you have a safe deposit box with a million dollars in it? The kid might tell me, "Oh, that's my front door key, my mom doesn't get home until 6:00." Right away, I would file that away. Some of that stuff is in their school records anyway. Single parent, momma works here until 5:00. If you need to reach her, you've got to call here because there's nobody home kind of thing. If I had a class of 30 kids, they all get groomed, they all think I'm a great guy. But maybe I've got a group of five or six

over here that I think are vulnerable that I'm also grooming even more than these other 25."

Setting up the opportunity

Sexual offenders will go to great lengths and exercise tremendous patience in an effort to satisfy their need to molest a child. They will use a variety of methods to setup the opportunity to molest a child, and will focus their efforts on "setting up" the child's parent, legal guardian or the whole family if necessary. Offenders have reported that before molesting a child their first priority is to gain the trust of the child's parent or caregiver.[18] They may help the family out financially by helping to pay for car repairs, house repairs, utility bills, clothes, food, or any other type of expense the family may have trouble with. The setup will sometimes extend beyond the family to the whole community. Offenders intentionally develop a reputation where everyone thinks they are a "nice guy."

Offender #1 comments on cultivating a "nice guy" image

> *"This is, you know, this is a good guy and he wouldn't do this kind of thing. And I do that by volunteering, working in the church. I was named Director of Summer Recreation down there at the end of that second year... Once I get them ready to follow me into the fire, then I just have to sit back and wait for an opportunity to come up. And it does, you know..."*

---

[18] Knight R. A., Carter D. L., U+ 0026 R. A. Prentky (1989). "A system for the classification of child molesters: Reliability and application". *Journal of Interpersonal Violence, 4*, 3-23.

After developing a trusting relationship with the victim's caregiver, offenders begin to develop a trusting relationship with their victim. Parents often warn children about strangers but the majority of sexual offenders are not strangers to the child. Children can become easy prey to someone they trust or is considered a "friend" of the family. It is a small percentage of offenders who are strangers to their victims. Offender surveys indicate that only 9% of offenders will attempt to approach a child to whom they are a stranger.[19]

Offender #8 explains why he did not molest children who were strangers to him.

> *"I never picked up a stranger off the street to molest. I felt safer with someone I knew because I used love as a weapon. I loved them. And all of my victims, that was something that they were looking for was love. And so I felt safer doing it that way; whereas to go out and solicit to pick up a child that doesn't know me, they're not going to have that fear of telling on me, that they're going to lose that love.*

> *"I would meet them one way or the other; it would be either through the parents, or I made a profession out of working with children. That put me in a position where I was very close to them, and also in a position where both the adults around me and the children trusted me with the kids... I started out volunteering in a child-care center. I was a Scout leader before that... I was a*

---

[19] Elliot, M., Browne, K., & Kilcoyne, J. (1995). Child sexual abuse prevention: What offenders tell us. Child Abuse and Neglect, 19, 579-594.

school bus driver as well as volunteering in the libraries of this parochial school... I would first get to know them to gain their trust. Play games with them... take them places... to a movie...roller skate... something that they would enjoy doing, and just gain their trust. Then... once I had their trust I would slowly move in, rubbing their back, going down touching their buttocks, rubbing their chest and letting my hand run down across their penis, and just gradually move up... I used the parents as well to gain their trust. What that does then is it takes the whole support system away from the child; Mom says he's a good person so, you know, he must be a good person. And then I think a lot of the victims then questioned, it must be me because everyone around me is saying he's a good person."

Sexual offenders can be very patient and spend months setting up the opportunity to sexually abuse a child. Some offenders have stated that they will simply wait for the opportunity to present itself. During one of my investigative interviews of an alleged sexual offender, I asked him, "Why do you think an adult would sexually touch a minor?" He responded by saying, "I guess it would have to be a matter of convenience, the time and the place were conducive to it." This is not the first thought that goes through the average person's mind when being asked this question. The first thought that comes to mind for most people is, "They must be sick, or some kind of a pervert!" However sexual offenders have a different perspective and view situations from a distorted way of thinking. The offender in this case was describing the circumstances he was in at the time he sexually assaulted his victim. He was alone with her in his back yard late at night when he sexually assaulted her.

As illustrated in the following case example, sexual offenders often have ulterior motives for what appears to be harmless friendly behavior. In this case, as in many cases, the parent and the child were victims of the offender's manipulations.

Case Example

A retired 65-year-old man was accused of molesting the three-year-old daughter of a woman he befriended on his walking route. The offender explained that he took a daily walk through the greenbelt of his neighborhood. One day he saw a young mother with her three-year-old daughter playing in their back yard and was immediately attracted to the three-year-old. So, he began his "setup." At first he would just smile and wave as he walked by. On one occasion he made a passing comment to the mother who was gardening in her back yard. After a few weeks they became friendly and she began to invite him into her yard. She would offer him a cool drink and they would discuss gardening. The victim's mother told investigators that the man appeared to be such a nice man, almost like a grandfather and she trusted him. She stated that her family lived out of state and she enjoyed having someone to talk to. He was the closest thing to a grandfather for her daughter. He began to stop by regularly to visit and gradually began to show more attention to her daughter. He was patiently waiting for the opportunity to be alone with her. After a few months the day finally came. During one of his visits Mom had to run some errands. He offered to stay with her daughter since he wasn't doing anything that afternoon. She agreed, and left to run her errands. Now that he had gained Mom's trust, he began to gain the trust of his victim. He began by tickling her and playing games she was interested in. While tickling her he would "accidentally" touch her private parts. Eventually he was given several other opportunities to baby-sit for her and the tickling escalated into a game he called "find the dollar in my pocket." He would cut out the bottom part of the pocket and when reaching in for the dollar the child would unintentionally touch his bare penis. He eventually started to put his hand inside of her clothes and began to fondle her. This went on for several months before the little girl told her mom about the games she had been playing with him.

Offender #5 explains how he set up his victims to molest them.

"It was a young boy that was delivering newspapers. When I saw him my first thought was that he was, you know, attractive. I would start talking to him. It was a slow process. You know, he'd come by and he'd collect once a month; I'd pay him. I would ask him if he would like to help around the house, make a little extra money, okay, and those things. So once he was there I'd always stop and pay attention to him, talk to him, and joke around with him, things like that, trying to be the good, the nice guy, gain his trust. Then I got closer to the mother, I found out that he was from a single-parent home. I befriended the mother. Eventually we started doing some other things, maybe go to a movie, something like that. And that process went on for I'd say three to four

months. Then he would come over more regularly. I would start talking to him about sexual things; and eventually I started molesting him."

Isolating the victim

After the offender has gained the trust of the victim's caregiver he will then begin to isolate his victim. Spending time alone with his victim allows the offender to develop an emotional relationship with the victim and gain their trust. Many offenders consider this time well spent because a victim who trusts them will be easier to manipulate and less likely to report the sexual abuse. Offenders may take their victims on outings to sporting events, skating, movies, and camping weekends or invite them for sleepovers. These outings not only help to develop a trusting relationship with their victim but also create an opportunity to molest them.

Offender #1 explains how he developed trust with the "victim of record".

"With April I started to help her with her schoolwork, and working on science projects and this kind of stuff. I set it up to where it looks better than it is because they were calling me. Saying, what are you doing? Do you got time? She's got a science project or something she needs help with, can you come over? I would be like, well I've got to do this and this, and maybe I, well maybe I can squeeze an hour in here somewhere. You know, I made it sound like it's a big deal but I really didn't have anything to do. When they asked me to come over I was thinking,

oh yeah, I'll get over there right now. I was trying to take it slow because I didn't want to get real crazy with it. So I would go and we would work on the schoolwork and mom and I would have a couple beers. Then I'd go home and that was the end of it. Then they started coming over to my house for barbecues. It got to the point where every time they came over she was always trailing me around. I was touching her in a non-sexual way. I would pat her on the back, put my hand on her shoulder or something. Basically what I was doing was getting her used to my touch, getting her used to being touched by me, having my hand on her. This went on for awhile, and it appeared harmless so nobody made any mention of it"

Offender #1 explains how he developed trust with the fourth grade students he molested.

"The kids all trusted me. They were all... I mean; these are all fourth graders, so they're like nine-ten years old. I always told people I thought fourth grade was the best age because they're old enough to not have to have you tie their shoes for them all the time, but they're young enough that they haven't learned to be sarcastic. They're still gullible enough that I could reel them in. It would be things like... when they'd come up with a skinned knee or whatever, you know, skinned elbows. I was always very tender with them, always concerned about them and never hurt them. This is one reason I think I got away with it for so long because I never hurt them. I never caused them physical pain."

After gaining the trust of the victim the offender is able to convince the victim that the sexual contact they are having is "OK and normal." If a child likes and trusts an adult they are more inclined to believe what the adult is telling them. In a study of 10-to 18-year-old victims the majority reported that when they were first abused, they did not know the sexual contact they had with the offender was wrong.[20] This may be one reason why some children fail to report the sexually abusive behavior. A child protection worker once told me that during an interview with a three-year-old girl she had asked her if her father had done anything "wrong" to her. The little girl replied, "No." Following this response the child protection worker asked her more specifically, "Did daddy make you put his tee-tee in your mouth?" She responded, "Yes." The abusive acts of a sexual offender are not only confusing to a young child but with older victims as well. The following comments were made by a twelve-year-old girl who was sexually abused by her stepfather.

> *"When I was 12 he would sometimes hug me and sometimes press against me with his penis, and you know, I liked it, you know, I didn't know it was wrong. When he would insert his finger in me he would say it's OK, it's normal, it's OK, and everyone goes through this. And you know those vibrators they have? I don't know where he got it, but he said this one was made for my age and that it's normal. Sometimes he would bargain me, sometimes if I would play with his....penis, he would buy me a CD or something like that, or I'd get a new outfit. Sometimes he would*

---

[20] Berliner, L., & Conte, J. R. (1990). The process of victimization: The victims' perspective. Child Abuse and Neglect, 14, 29-40.